We Recovered Too

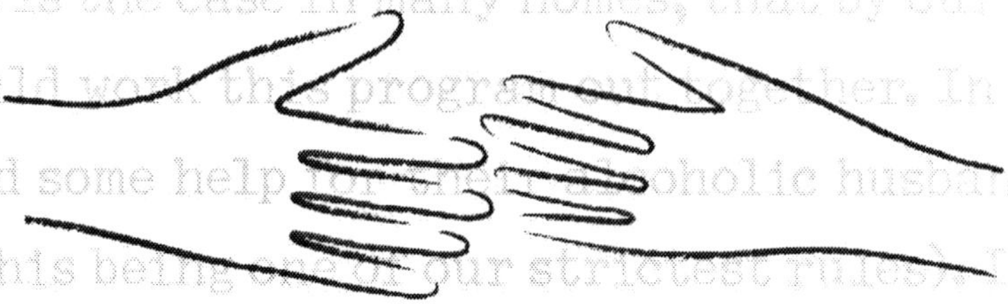

HAZELDEN®

We Recovered Too

The Family Groups' Beginnings
in the Pioneers' Own Words

....

Hazelden Celebrates

Al-Anon's 60th Anniversary

MICHAEL FITZPATRICK

Hazelden
Center City, Minnesota 55012
hazelden.org

LIBRARY OF CONGRESS CATALOGING-IN-PUBLICATION DATA

Fitzpatrick, Michael, 1959–
    We recovered too : the family groups' beginnings in the pioneers' own words / Michael Fitzpatrick.
        p.   cm.
    Includes bibliographical references.
    ISBN 978-1-61649-165-9
        1. Al-Anon Family Group Headquarters, Inc.   2. Alcoholics—Family relationships.   3. Alcoholics—Rehabilitation.   I. Title.
    HV5132.F49 2011
    362.292'3—dc23

                                                    2011028533

EDITOR'S NOTE
In keeping with the Eleventh and Twelfth Traditions of Alcoholic Anonymous and Al-Anon, first names with initials for last names are used for people in both memberships.

Alcoholics Anonymous, AA, the Big Book, the *Grapevine, AA Grapevine,* and *GV* are registered trademarks of Alcoholics Anonymous World Services, Inc.

Permission statements appear on page 217.

15 14 13 12 11   1 2 3 4 5 6

Cover design by David Spohn
Interior design by Cathy Spengler
Typesetting by BookMobile

Legacy 12

Bringing AA and Twelve Step History Alive

Hazelden's *Legacy 12* publishing initiative enriches people's recovery with dynamic multimedia works that use rare original-source documents to bring Alcoholics Anonymous and Twelve Step history alive.

This book is dedicated to the three most important women in my life:

- *My mother, Mary, for her prayers, her love, and her example.*
- *My daughter, Emily, with her contagious smile and positive attitude.*
- *My wife, Joy, without whom none of this would happen—she makes it all worth it.*

Contents

Foreword

IT'S BEEN SIXTY YEARS since Lois W. and Anne B. wrote the first Al-Anon–related letters in the library of Stepping Stones, Bill and Lois Wilson's historic home in Bedford Hills, New York. Today, loved ones who suffer the effects of alcoholism on the family can find hope through Al-Anon Family Groups. Lois started the Stepping Stones Foundation in 1979 to make the history of AA and Al-Anon available. In this book, Mike Fitzpatrick honors Lois's intentions with respect and dignity. It has been my sincere pleasure to offer the Stepping Stones Archives to help him tell these stories. It is a tribute to Mike's diligence that the information in this book from the Stepping Stones Archives is appearing in print for the first time ever.

Stepping Stones keeps and preserves the historic records of Bill and Lois W., respective cofounders of Alcoholics Anonymous and Al-Anon Family Groups. The Stepping Stones Archives show that Lois began to practice the principles of AA in her life as a family member in 1936. By 1951, she was happy working in the garden, being a homemaker, and helping drunks and their families. Bill's persistence helped Lois to see that family members needed a clearinghouse similar to AA. Bill convinced Lois that she was the person to take on the challenge. Lois went on to dedicate her life to enthusiastically nurturing the movement.

Of course, hundreds of women and men worked alongside Lois in her endeavor. This book introduces us to a few of them. Lois's relationship with the first recovering family member she ever met, Anne S., is finally discussed in these pages. A talk to the Family

Groups by Bill W., which demonstrates his influence on Al-Anon, is also included (see chapter 8). In my opinion, this is one of Bill's most eloquent talks.

Some of the most meaningful experiences I've had at Stepping Stones have been the hours spent with Mike, pondering connections between historic figures, determining how best to make the words of Bill, Lois, and others available, and reveling in what the past means in the present. While Stepping Stones commemorates the achievements specifically of Bill and Lois in the field of recovery from alcoholism, this book commemorates the achievements of all the key people in the Family Group recovery movement. Without Anne S., Margaret D., Pearl E., Bertha M., and the others portrayed here, hope for recovery for alcoholics and their families might not be as possible as it is today.

Lois W. believed that Al-Anon would be equal to, if not rival, AA in membership and effectiveness. Yet many loved ones of alcoholics continue to suffer. Books such as this will help more family members find and celebrate recovery, while also informing and inspiring many other readers. The language of suffering and hope is universal.

With this work, Mike Fitzpatrick has proven to be a faithful friend to Stepping Stones and the recovery community. His respect for the founders and pioneers of the Family Group movement is reflected in his commitment to letting them tell their stories, as much as possible, in their own words. I thank him for preserving this valuable history and sharing it with the world.

Annah Perch
Executive Director
Stepping Stones, the historic home of Bill and Lois W.

Preface

IN THE BOOK *ALCOHOLICS ANONYMOUS,* Bill W. wrote, "Remember that we deal with alcohol—cunning, baffling, powerful! Without help it is too much for us."[1] As baffling as alcohol is to the alcoholic, the effects and destructiveness of alcoholism on non-alcoholic family members are equally or possibly even more baffling.

Over the past sixty years, Al-Anon Family Groups has grown into a worldwide fellowship with groups in 133 countries outside the United States and Canada. Including Alateen, the groups number more than 25,000 worldwide, and Al-Anon literature is available in forty languages. The groups have had a positive impact on the lives of countless thousands of people suffering from the devastation of alcoholism.

When it was suggested that I do something related to Al-Anon's history in celebration of Al-Anon Family Groups sixtieth anniversary, I was honored and excited to be able to use resources I already had at hand for such a project. In 2005, I acquired the audio library that originally belonged to Arbutus O., one of Al-Anon's pioneering members. She and her husband, Bill, lived in Texas. They began recording AA and Al-Anon conferences and events in the early fifties. They were also able to locate recordings and other memorabilia from founding members dating back to the late 1940s. Together, these materials comprise the Midwest Tape Library, now in my possession.

Arbutus had only one condition or request when I was preparing over three thousand reel-to-reel tapes for the journey to my home in Arizona. She asked that I make the recordings available for the next generation of AA and Al-Anon members. Since that time, I have dedicated hundreds of hours and a great many personal resources to having the audio library digitized, and I have set up a website to make the recordings available as they become ready. (To learn more, visit the website www.recoveryspeakers.org.) In addition to the thousands of audio recordings, I also have hundreds of historical documents. These letters, journals, and other text sources are known as the Fitzpatrick Archive. Therefore, in this book's Notes section, most citations refer to these three sources—the Midwest Tape Library, the Fitzpatrick Archive, and www.recoveryspeakers.org, also known as the Recovery Speakers Library.

I began to think about the best way to use the audio recordings and other archives in my possession to honor both Arbutus's request and Al-Anon's anniversary. The biggest challenge was deciding what material to use and what not to use. I didn't want to tell the same story that had been told in other publications; however, the reality is, there's really only one history to tell.

Consequently, I decided to tell the story in a way that had never been done before—I decided to select recordings of several Al-Anon pioneers and the cofounders and let them tell the Al-Anon story "in their own words." This would give me the opportunity to use some rare recordings of the early days of the Family Groups as content for both a book and an audio CD. For example, I have a recording made at the First AA International Convention held in 1950, where the "wives' group" from Toronto was invited to share at a session. I've included transcriptions of their talks in the chapter entitled "Sound Homes." Another transcription is from a record album of Bill Wilson talking to a wives' group in Salt Lake City. Both of these historical talks had been stored away, unreleased for many years.

In addition to the audio recordings, I wanted to include some of the documents found in the many boxes of archives I received from Arbutus as well as other interesting pieces I'd picked up along the way. These archives are comprised of old letters, memos, typed speeches, and notebooks. One thing I was particularly excited about sharing was a letter written by Al-Anon pioneer Myrtle L. about the time she visited with Henrietta D., the wife of AA number three, Bill D. Henrietta's candid recollections of the early days of AA and those early wives' meetings with Anne S. are remarkable.

When I began writing, I immediately knew that any historical look at Al-Anon couldn't just begin with its official organization in 1951 as "The Clearing House." The book had to include those very early days of Alcoholics Anonymous when the wives joined their husbands at AA meetings and then later began to meet separately to discuss their own problems. I felt it was necessary to show how Al-Anon was born out of Alcoholics Anonymous.

The first chapter, "855 Ardmore Avenue," tells the story of Anne S., the wife of AA's cofounder Dr. Bob. As you read on, you will meet many other people who share their part in the formation of the Family Groups. There is an entire chapter of historic *AA Grapevine* articles written by Family Group members both before and after Al-Anon began.

The book shows how individual family members (usually the wives of alcoholics) recognized that they, too, were suffering and needed a program for recovery. It also details some original versions of the Steps used by the wives' groups in overcoming their problems. These groups sprang up throughout the United States and Canada and eventually became what is known today as Al-Anon Family Groups.

The combination of audio transcriptions, rare articles, and documents allowed me to tell a fact-filled story of how Al-Anon got its start, as well as many of the early successes and challenges facing the organization. I tried to incorporate as much information as I could about the important characters involved in the founding of Al-Anon, including both cofounders. Thanks to the generosity of the Stepping Stones Archives, I was also able to include some never-before-published letters.

Throughout the book I attempted to limit my personal comments and to use the material available to create a work that delivers on the promise of telling this story "in their own words." Along with the stories of the founders, the last two chapters feature personal stories of two current Al-Anon members. They tell how their lives changed as the result of Al-Anon Family Groups. It's interesting to note that the story of Al-Anon may at times sound a bit different when told by different people. I believe this occurs because each person has a unique perspective on the events based on personal experiences.

It was my goal from the beginning to adhere strictly to the Twelve Traditions of Al-Anon, and I have been very careful to protect the anonymity of individual members. I have always had deep respect for Al-Anon Family Groups and the members who have done so much for so many. Of course, Al-Anon World Service Office (WSO) does not endorse any literature that is not "Al-Anon conference approved" and the Traditions suggest that Al-Anon has no opinion on outside issues.

Accompanying the print edition of *We Recovered Too* is a CD that contains the voices from the transcriptions included in the text. Unfortunately, it wasn't possible to include all of the recordings used in the research and writing of the book. However, the CD contains a representative selection from the talks used. An e-book is also available that contains audio clips from the transcriptions.

I hope you will find this work both informative and entertaining.

Acknowledgments

I AM VERY GRATEFUL to Sid Farrar for our many conversations that ultimately led to the writing of this book. When he shared that Hazelden wanted to recognize and celebrate Al-Anon's sixtieth anniversary with this publication, I was thrilled!

Since the actual writing of the book needed to be completed within a very short time to make its 2011 debut, I am most thankful to my family, who stood by me all the way. Their support was unwavering as I frantically dug through recordings and paperwork to shape this book.

I want to thank my friend, author William Borchert, for opening the door to Hazelden and this new career. He supplied lots of encouragement throughout the process of coauthoring *1000 Years of Sobriety*, my first writing effort. He has continued to offer his encouragement and support.

I also want to thank Aaron and Vannoy for their contributions. It is impossible for me to thank by name everyone who has supported and encouraged me in this effort. However, Howard P. and Tom I., two of my closest mentors, were always on call and had just the right thing to say when I needed lifting up.

Lastly, my heartfelt thanks to Annah Perch and the Stepping Stones Board for allowing me access to their incredible archives. Without their cooperation this book would never have been written.

Guide to the Audio CD

The sixteen-track CD included with this book offers highlights from archival recordings of Al-Anon's early leaders: passages from speeches, interviews, and other sources. Over thirty hours of recordings were excerpted and adapted for inclusion in the book *We Recovered Too*. While the CD contains some of this audio, it does not parallel the book exactly and is not intended as a "listen-along" disk. Instead, it serves as a collection of personal accounts and reflections told in these visionaries' own words—stories that, together, capture the spirit of the Family Groups.

Audio Tracks

Total running time: approx. 78 minutes

1. Bob S. Jr., son of Dr. Bob & Anne S., recalls his mother in a recorded statement, 1975. (5:17)
2. Bill W. discusses his spiritual experience, radio interview, June 1956. (6:15)
3. Anne S. records a brief message to Lois and Bill W. on a wire recorder at her home in Akron, OH, June 29, 1947 (the only known record of her voice). (:53)
4. Myrtle L. discusses the early family groups, Twelfth Southeastern Regional AA Convention, Biloxi, MS, Aug. 24, 1956. (4:24)
5. Edith B. speaks on "Teamwork in the Home," First International Convention of AA, Cleveland, OH, July 29, 1950. (6:32)

6. Margaret D. tells her story, Fifth Al-Anon Rally, Detroit, MI, Feb. 23, 1964. (5:25)

7. Margaret D. describes alcoholism as a disease, Fifth Al-Anon Rally, Detroit, MI, Feb. 24, 1964. (1:49)

8. Margaret D. recalls her first Al-Anon meeting, Fifth Al-Anon Rally, Detroit, MI, Feb. 24, 1964. (5:15)

9. Margaret D. discusses the challenge of the Twelfth Step, Fifth Al-Anon Rally, Detroit, MI, Feb. 23, 1964. (4:46)

10. Lois W. speaks about her early days with Bill at the Twelfth Southeastern Regional AA Convention, Biloxi, MS, Aug. 24, 1956. (7:40)

11. Lois W. recounts the end of Bill's drinking, Twelfth Southeastern Regional AA Convention, Biloxi, MS, Aug. 24, 1956. (4:20)

12. Lois W. tells the shoe-throwing story, Twelfth Southeastern Regional AA Convention, Biloxi, MS, Aug. 24, 1956. (3:05)

13. Bill W.'s encouragement speech to a "wives' group" in Salt Lake City, UT, June 1951. (6:32)

14. Lois W. tells the "rowboat story" in a speech at a recovery event in Topeka, KS, Oct. 17, 1975. (6:48)

15. Lois W. recounts realizing that "I needed this for myself" in a speech at a recovery event in Topeka, KS, Oct. 17, 1975. (5:21)

16. Anne B. speaks at a DARR conference, a recovery event in Palm Springs, CA, June 4, 1983. (3:34)

Author's Note: Especially noteworthy are several tracks that recently resurfaced after being all but lost for many years. These include track 2, from an interview with Bill W.; track 4, the only known recording of Anne S.'s voice; track 5, a "wives' meeting" speech by Edith B., the wife of a Toronto AA member; tracks 10–12, from a speech by Al-Anon cofounder Lois W., and track 13, from a 1951 speech by Bill W.—a speech recorded and printed onto a record album once owned by Bill and Lois W and likely the only such copy.

Please also note that the CD includes some passages that do not appear in the book itself.

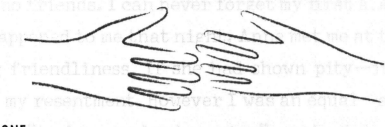

ONE

855 Ardmore Avenue:
The Story of Anne S.

ill W., the cofounder of Alcoholics Anonymous, referred to Anne S. as "the mother of our first group, Akron."[1] As you read her story, you will learn of a woman who possessed a deep faith in God and unwavering love for those who suffer, much as a mother feels for her children. Her friends and family were always ready to tell people what her contributions were to the founding of both AA and the Al-Anon Family Groups. She was able to adapt simple, spiritual principles into her daily living and her giving. Many of her principles are reflected in the Twelve Steps, which had their beginnings in her home, 855 Ardmore Avenue, Akron, Ohio.

In two interviews, in 1975 and 2001, Bob Jr., the son of Dr. Bob and Anne, shared comments about his mother. The following account is adapted from excerpts of these recorded interviews.

• • • • • • • • • • • • •

Anne was born in Oak Park, Illinois, one of four children. Her father was of modest circumstances and worked for the Santa Fe Railroad. Anne attended public schools and graduated from Wellesley College. She was always quick to explain that she attended on a scholarship because otherwise the school was beyond the family's means. She taught school for a few years prior to marrying Dr. Bob.

Mother was completely unassuming, deeply in love with Dad, and their love always showed. She did not drink at all, although one time she took me and my sister aside and told us that she was going to act like she was drunk when Dad got home so we were to support her. She put on the worst show of a drunk I'd ever seen! It was embarrassing to me, to my dad, and to my sister; she did a terrible job of acting like a drunk. Anyway, she was so desperate that she tried stuff like that. She took up smoking at the age of fifty-five and explained to me that if I waited until I was fifty-five to smoke she wouldn't criticize me.[2]

Mother was a deeply, quietly religious person. Each day she had her own "quiet time" (as she put it) for communication with the Lord. At that time alcoholics were not welcomed at hospitals if they could afford it, which most of them couldn't, so many came into our home and were treated there. Now the treatment fell to Mother's lot because Dad was off to work each day. She had many, many experiences with drunks just coming out of stupors—including being chased around the house with her own butcher knife and people sliding down the drain spouts to search for more alcohol. She remained unflappable throughout with a deep faith and abiding love for these derelicts and their families. But she soon reached the point where it was very difficult to shock her anymore.

Some stayed for months and were accepted as part of the family—Archie was with us over a year. They shared in what we had and Mother was their daytime mentor. Her serenity among these circumstances bred serenity among the alcoholics. Her counseling was done quietly and selflessly. She never lost faith in these guys. Of course, she was the one who was cooking the meals, making the beds, and cleaning up the messes. She was also the one on the telephone answering the inquirers as the word began to trickle out. She made everyone who stayed there have a quiet time in the morning when they might feel nearer to God—this was a requirement which involved some reading of the Bible and study. It was one of her rules.

AA wasn't an instant success, and it was thought of as a "cult" or "a bunch of nuts" and Mom endured all the snubs. We got kicked out of the Presbyterian Church on account of AA, so it must have been very difficult for her but she never lost faith.

At AA meetings she always sat in the back of the room and always put newcomers at ease by quietly greeting them. She bore the poverty of the times without complaint and spent virtually nothing on herself.

In later life her eyesight failed to the point where she could just distinguish movement across the room. One operation for removal of cataracts was a failure, so she would not permit an operation on the other as she said she still had some vision and believed that was better than none. Only after she was gone did it dawn on me that this deep, considerate, quiet person who would do battle for what she believed or to protect our family was the solid foundation that Dr. Bob needed to carry on his part of AA.[3] ⌒

THE STORY OF ANNE and her influence on AA and the Al-Anon Family Groups began on a Saturday afternoon, May 11, 1935, when she received a phone call from an acquaintance she had met at the local Oxford Group meeting. A nondenominational Christian movement, the Oxford Group had begun in 1921 and grown rapidly throughout the world. Anne had been attending Oxford Group meetings with her husband, Dr. Bob, hoping that he might somehow find a way to stop drinking.

Up to that point, both she and Dr. Bob had tried everything

available to them to get him to stop drinking, but as Dr. Bob later said, "I just kept getting tight every night." Dr. Bob's drinking was continuous and had completely gotten out of hand. They were on the brink of losing their Akron, Ohio, home and his medical practice.

This particular May afternoon was the eve of Mother's Day, and Dr. Bob had come home with a potted plant. While the beautiful spring plant sat on the table, he was passed out drunk upstairs. The phone rang and it was Henrietta Seiberling from the Oxford Group. Henrietta was excited about a visitor from New York who might be able to help Dr. Bob with his drinking problem. His name was Bill W.

Bill, a businessman, had recently found the answer to his alcoholic problem. As part of his own recovery, he was trying to help others. He had been sober for five months, but on this day his sobriety was a bit shaky. Bill had just concluded several days of intense business meetings in what turned out to be an unsuccessful proxy battle to gain interest in a company. If the meetings had been successful, he would have been back on his feet financially and would have likely been named president of the company.

But the meetings had failed and all that was left was a dim flicker of hope that somehow Bill might be able to salvage the deal in the coming weeks. He was broke, discouraged, and alone at the Mayflower Hotel in Akron with not even enough money to get back home to New York. This had been Bill's first real opportunity to reclaim his successful business status since sobering up.

Just five months earlier, in December 1934, Bill had been lying in a bed at Towns Hospital on Central Park West. He recalled his experience in a 1956 recorded interview: "My wife was downstairs talking with the doctor. I had been there before; it was the end of a long road. And she was asking the doctor why I couldn't stop drinking and the good man was obliged to tell her that I had an obsession of the mind that condemned me to drink against my will, a sensitivity to the body which he called an allergy, so that if the drinking was continued I would be destined to go mad or die. In fact, he told her frankly that she would soon have to lock me up if my life is to be saved. It was the end of the road and I knew it. I was a hopeless alcoholic and in those days the chance of recovery was rated at one, two, or three percent."[4]

During this hospital stay, Bill had a "profound spiritual experience." In the same interview, he described the experience this way:

> *My friend visited me there. At first I was suspicious. I was afraid I was going to be evangelized again. I asked him what his simple little formula was. Again he repeated it.* "Get honest with yourself. Confess your faults. Make amends to those you've harmed. Try to help other people without any thought of reward, and pray to whatever God you think there is—if only as an experiment." *It was just as simple, yet just as mysterious, as that. When he had gone, I fell into a terrific depression and in the bottom of that depression I cried out even as a small child might, "IF THERE IS A GOD, WILL HE SHOW HIMSELF!"*
>
> *Instantly the place lit up electric white. It seemed to me that I stood on the top of a mountain, a great wind was blowing, which I have realized was not of air but of spirit. When the ecstasy subsided, I lay on the bed. It seemed to me that I was now in a new world where everything was all right. A great peace settled over me.*[5]

Bill went on to say that he was instantly released of the obsession to drink and had not been seriously tempted since.

Bill worked frantically to try to sober up alcoholics in the New York City area while attending Oxford Group meetings with his wife, Lois. He would call on alcoholics at the hospital and take them home. At times this work was discouraging because none of them were staying sober. Bill was so enlightened by his own spiritual experience that he felt others should become enlightened in the same way.

He recalled what his doctor, William Silkworth, had suggested: "Bill, you can soften these people up if you will pour it into them how hopeless this really is—an obsession of the mind which condemns one to drink and an allergy that condemns one to go mad or die. Why don't you throw that dose into them first and then maybe they will buy this moral psychology of yours."[6]

Bill now paced the lobby of the Mayflower Hotel, feeling discouraged by the failed business meetings. He was likely homesick as well, from being away from Lois. At one end of the lobby was a bar and at the other end a church directory. Bill said this was the first real temptation he had experienced since sobering up. He knew he needed someone right then or he might drink.

Bill selected a name from the church directory and made the call that led to a meeting that very afternoon with Henrietta Seiberling, a non-alcoholic member of the Oxford Group. When he arrived at her house, he told her his story and his need to talk to another alcoholic.

Henrietta was excited and wanted to get Bill and Dr. Bob together right away. She felt this might be the answer to her and Anne's prayers. She called over to Dr. Bob's house and learned through Anne that he was in no condition to meet with anyone that day. Anne promised to have him over to Henrietta's the following day.

On May 12, 1935, Mother's Day, Anne and Dr. Bob arrived at the Seiberling estate's gatehouse, where Henrietta was living. This is where Dr. Bob and Bill W., the cofounders of AA, met for the first time. Bob Jr. drove his mother and father to the meeting and he had this to say about his father on that day: "He had a terrible hangover and finally he said, 'Okay, fifteen minutes of this bird is all I want.' But folks, when we got there he and Bill went off to a room by themselves and it wasn't fifteen minutes; they stayed several hours. And as a result of that meeting and at my mother's invitation, Bill came to live at our home there in Akron, Ohio, for all that summer—a three-month period of time. This was the time and the place when Alcoholics Anonymous was first started."[7]

Bob Jr., who became a member of Al-Anon many years later, spoke about growing up in the family home and would often mention that they had very little, that alcoholism and the economic times had reduced them to poverty. He said that if it hadn't been for the mortgage moratorium declared by President Franklin Roosevelt, they would have lost their home.

Bob Jr.'s first wife, Betty, spoke fondly of her mother-in-law: "The most important thing about Anne was that she was a sheltered place for people in trouble. In any given week I doubt that any minister could have counseled more people, prayed with more people.

In times of trouble, so many people rushed to her. She was a rock, a comforter through God's help. So many of us loved her; she was truly a person who went placidly amid the noise and haste."[8]

Anne's work with alcoholics and their families in the earliest days of AA set the example for what would later become the Al-Anon Family Groups. By the mid-1940s, solid groups of AA wives and families had begun gathering for more than just support of their alcoholic husbands.

Lois W., Bill's wife and the cofounder of Al-Anon, spoke of Anne when recalling the summer of 1935.

....

Annie invited me out there for my vacation. I loved Annie from the minute I saw her. She not only had a heart as big as all outdoors, but it contained great wisdom. She was able to quickly put her finger on the crux of any matter and both the alcoholic and his wife sought her advice. Bob's tireless work with alcoholics at the hospital brought numbers of them to Akron to be hospitalized. After their treatment, Annie and Bob would take many of them in for a more or less protracted stay at their home.

Hosts of groups sprang from this contact and in these early groups both married partners were indefatigable in working with alcoholics and their wives. I wonder if you realize how slow AA grew in the beginning. By 1939, there were only one hundred members and a handful of groups, but as the numbers swelled, members of the older groups visited as many of the new as possible.

Bill and I were freer to do more of this traveling than were Annie and Bob. Wherever we visited, there was always an opportunity for Annie and me to talk to the local wives. We always told these newer mates how we had found that we also needed AA's Twelve Steps. Most of us felt a desire even from the beginning to get together and discuss our side of the alcohol problem and to search for ways for our own development.[9] ⤙

EVEN THOUGH Al-Anon Family Groups didn't officially begin until June 1951—two years after Anne died—it is unquestionable that she was an inspiration for Al-Anon's development. Many of the early wives and husbands wrote letters after Anne died in June 1949, describing their memories and experiences with Anne. The following is a sampling of these letters.[10] The impact Anne's life had on these AA members and their families is clearly demonstrated in the words of her friends.

· · · · · · · · · · · · ·

On Friday night when I went to the house on Ardmore Avenue I met the most thoughtful, understanding person I have ever known. After talking with her a while, I addressed her as Mrs. S_____ and she said; "Anne to you, my dear."

Anne taught me to have a "quiet time" in the morning that I might feel near to God and receive strength for the day. She taught me to surrender my husband to God and not to try to tell him how to stay sober, as I had tried that and failed. Anne taught me to love everyone. She said, "Ask yourself, what is wrong with me today if I don't love you?" She said, "The love of God is triangular. It must flow from God through me, through you, and back to God."

In the early part of 1936 Anne organized a "women's group" for wives of alcoholics, whereby in her loving way she tried to teach us patience, love, and unselfishness. When I met and talked with this intelligent deeply spiritual woman I was completely sold on A.A.

—Henrietta D.

I was a cynical, despairing wife of a hopeless alcoholic. In order to assuage my total unhappiness I had carefully tried to destroy within myself all feeling, all longing, and all beauty. I had no friends.

I can never forget my first A.A. meeting—a miracle happened to me that night. Anne met me at the door with disarming friend-

liness. If she had shown pity, it would have increased my resentment. However I was an equal—someone to be loved. Anne "took me under her wing" as she did all the wives preceding me and hundreds more to follow.

Anne was gentle but she was direct. In the weeks to follow, I eagerly visited with my new-found friends at each meeting. Anne came to me one night and said, "Dorothy, everyone has been so kind to you, never forget that and never forget to welcome the newcomers as you were welcomed." I have tried to follow that.

I can still hear her chuckle. I can still hear her say, "My dear, I am so glad to see you."

As I sit here looking at her picture I wish that all wives of alcoholics could have known her. I wish they could know the joy to be found in friendliness to the new member. I wish they could feel the great adventure of casting away self-pity and realize the pleasure of loving others.

⎯ Dorothy

In the days when no one could afford a hospital, in the days when her own kitchen was a battlefield where with prayer and hot coffee and good fellowship and still more hot coffee, a soul was encouraged to go forth and make a fresh stand against liquor, "because this time you're not alone." Anne was the chief against despondency and despair.

Think back now to those struggling days of 1935. Bill and Dr. Bob and some others would probably tell you that for a time Anne literally was Alcoholics Anonymous. The transition from family group to national organization was in vast degree her accomplishment.

She knew what was the right thing to do and had the courage to do it. Intuitively she began to set up each new convert as a friend, and yet as a separate and distinct unit. People write of her now as if, though departed, she still is with them. That was Anne's special message. "Carry God in your heart. Walk where you will walk with the knowledge that your friends are near you," she counseled. She planted self-confidence in people's hearts and imparted the secret of her own unquestioning faith. It is a reservoir of hope that those who use it find adequate and never-failing.

As with the young man from a distant city who lived for ten months in Anne and Dr. Bob's home. "At first I knew in my heart that nothing would ever persuade me to go back to my home city," he writes. "After six months with Dr. Bob and Anne I realized I must go back to the same place where I had fouled up. Anne didn't tell me so. She helped me see myself in the right light so the decision came to me slowly and naturally." Let us add permanently.

Sometimes the miracle that Anne affected took place more simply. A handshake at an A.A. meeting, an introduction to various friends, perhaps a visit to the home—no one kept any count. Anne did no preaching, but she sometimes wrapped a key message up in a neat package. "People have been good to you here," she told one. "Be sure that you go out of your way to extend a welcome to newcomers whenever you meet them."

People speak of her knowing how to say the right thing in just the right way. To a newcomer, case-hardened, fearful of facing embarrassment, negative in her thinking, because she has seen her drinking husband "reformed" before and was dubious about the whole thing she said merely, "We are all here for the same purpose. Everything will be all right." And everything was all right.

But it was in the greater and still unknown field of the human soul that Anne effected her works. From that fateful day in 1935 when A.A. took shape in the persons of Bill W. and Dr. Bob, both uncertain as to what each could do for himself but both determined to help the other, she saw her field of usefulness and seized it. No man or woman is powerful enough to defeat alcoholism unaided, but any sincere alcoholic can help rescue some other alcoholic, and in the saving win himself freedom. That was the program, and with God's aid and her husband's tremendous power—he was and is a big man, a man of deep voice and great-ness of spirit—she set herself to extend this program to reach thousands who asked to be freed from the slavery of drink.

Truly her soul goes marching on.

—F.B.B.

I shall always remember Anne. It was at the Kings School meet-ing that I first met this remarkable woman. Being a stranger there, I can still remember her coming over and talking to me. She inquired if it was my first meeting and I remember the genu-ine interest she showed concerning me, and my efforts to learn about this way of life.

It was February 1948 that I planned to go to New Mexico for three weeks or so. As Dr. Bob and Anne were going to New Mexico also it was mutually agreed that I would drive their car as Anne was not well. She and Dr. Bob would go by train and we would turn the car over to them at Clovis, New Mexico.

We were caught in a very bad blizzard and had an accident damaging the rear fender and bumper. A garage man estimated the damage at less than $50.00 but could not repair the car due to lack of parts and so we continued the rest of the trip with deep misgivings—heart sick wishing it could have been our own car. We met Dr. Bob and Anne at the station in Clovis and immedi-ately told them the bad news. Dr. Bob asked simply, "How bad is it" and was told, "Not too bad doctor." We walked to the car—Anne reassuring my wife—asking about our trip—how she felt—and showed no apparent concern about the car.

When we reached the car the good doctor saw it [the damage], smiled, and said, "I could've done better than that." Anne chuckled and said, "Oh that's nothing, the doctor has done worse than that." Immediately—when she chuckled—we both felt relieved of our tension.

—Gabe

It was a great privilege to become acquainted with Anne in December nineteen hundred and forty-one. At that time we were attending our second AA Meeting and Dr. Bob was the speaker. That evening in Toledo, Ohio, somehow or other by more than a coincidence I believe, we were among a few who were invited to meet Doctor Bob and Anne after the meeting. Anne was so sympathetic and interested in us that we loved her immediately and from that time on our friendship strengthened through the years.

Anne, to me, was much more than a friend. She represented something so fine and came the closest to being a spiritual body of any person I ever hope to know.

During the time when her eyes were failing so rapidly she did not seem to be filled with fear as so many of us would have been. Instead, she had those spiritual qualities which enabled her to adjust to the situation so beautifully and continued to be so interested in and thoughtful of others. She was so cheerful throughout the operations, even though the outcome was doubtful, that I thought her philosophy must have been:

The inner side of every cloud
Is bright and shining
And so — I turn my clouds about,
And always wear them inside out —
To show the lining.
  — Myrtle

There never seemed to be a striving for self-glory or a "setting herself up as an authority." Rather I got the impression of a precious wonder and thankfulness, that in her way she could be one of God's channels in sharing with others the soul satisfaction and peace which she had found.

May we be very careful not to saddle Ann's personality with the deadliest of all our errors that can hold mankind back from spiritual growth — namely spiritual pride. May we loose her in our consciousness so that she may continue on in her kind, loving, understanding and humble way, working only for the Glory of God, which will hasten her full enlightenment and experience of The Divine.

⸻Ruth G.

Anne had a wonderful sense of humor. At one time, I had told her about a Unity affirmation that I had learned which was as follows: "In God I Am Forever Undisturbed." One evening when business conditions were pressing me very hard and I felt the need of quiet and good company, my wife and I went over to visit Anne and Bob. Upon entering the living room, Anne was quietly sitting in her chair in the corner near the fireplace and in her keen sense of humor, looked up at me and said, "Good evening Roland, I assume that in God you are very much undisturbed." Of course, this immediately broke the ice and settled me down to an ease of feeling at home with friends.

Anne was most unselfish. Many an A.A. spent weeks, even many months in her home and she gave of her time in helping to answer the questions that would come from an addled alcoholic mind. Her patience was unlimited.

Anne was good for the alcoholic's wife. Her broad understanding of being the wife of an alcoholic enriched her with qualities that radiated hope for the other wives. I can recall very well one experience my own wife had with Anne. Dorothy had a rather caustic sense of humor and Anne told her, "Anytime that you make fun at another one's expense, that is not humor." This again was keen insight Anne had in the psychology of living.

⸻Roland

THIS NEXT LETTER I share in its entirety simply because it clearly captures the times in which AA was founded as well as the contributions Anne made to both alcoholics and their wives.

• • • • • • • • • • • •

My husband was 34 and an alcoholic. Other people drank normally. My husband got drunk.

*I was eternally on the defensive. I couldn't read. I couldn't
listen to good music. I couldn't enjoy anything.*

*I tried to appear busy. I tried to avoid crowds. Put us at
a party and either Joe would get drunk and pass out, which
was preferable, or he'd start pawing the women, which was
humiliating.*

*I felt as if I was 200 years old. All 200 years were weighing
down when a friend of ours—this was 12 years ago (1937) and
A.A. hadn't gained much reputation—persuaded Joe to attend a
meeting of Alcoholics in Akron.*

*To myself I said between gritted teeth, "I'll be hanged if I want
to associate with a bunch of drunks and their broken-down hag-
gard wives."*

Then that first meeting . . .

*I had lived on the surface for years. I could show a surface
kindliness, but I was bitter and resentful inside.*

*The meeting was in somebody's home. I halted on the thresh-
old that first evening, hesitant, fearful, not knowing what might
be ahead. I doubted the whole occasion. This was Joe's affair! If it
would bring about his sobriety, O.K.—but it was not for me. I felt
I didn't need it.*

*Further, I rather enjoyed the hard shell I had built around
myself. No one could hurt me further. I had been shamed and
ostracized and pitied. I was proof against further hurt.*

*And then this greeting, "Come in, my dear." It was Anne Smith,
as gracious, as friendly, as charming as any woman I had ever
met or known.*

*If she had pitied me, I would have fled in anger and disgrace.
She was wise enough to know that. She understood. She knew
that most wives of alcoholics feel fear. But you couldn't be afraid
with Anne.*

*That love of Anne's changed things. For me it was like the
miracle coming to Paul on the road to Damascus. That night
when I reached home I got down on my knees and prayed. I
wanted to be different.*

My parents had always been normally religious. I had never been anything other than religious. But this was different.

When anything of a memorial tribute is printed about Anne, I hope it emphasizes this big point; she didn't want glorification for glory's sake. She would have hoped only to tell other wives how to carry on.

She knew how to handle the wife of an alcoholic. She knew the days and nights full of despair, the poverty-stricken effort to keep up appearances, the unsatisfactory blending of shabbiness and hard pride.

Time after time I saw her melt some other person's heart.

A proud woman, a hard shelled woman, walked in belligerently. She had her speech all prepared. "Well, Mrs. Smith," she began belligerently—

"Call me Anne, my dear."

That love cracked the proud one, won her over.

Anne was a good listener. She knew the therapy of getting things off your chest.

Things might have grown into an old story. But not with her. Every meeting with a newcomer was a fresh experience. She greeted strangers and listened for their names. Next time she'd be able to call them by name.

In these early days there were no women alcoholics in the group. They were just wives—those who still had wives.

Bill emphasizes that in those days—1935, 1936, 1937—we few people were clinging together like a little group of persons saved from a shipwreck.

In those early days most of us didn't have telephones. We were handed a little address book. We were told "All our homes are open to you. Drop in at any time."

We did!

Many a time Joe and I dropped in on Dr. Bob and Anne for a pot-luck meal. We might have bread and milk for supper. We might have corned beef hash for Sunday. There were no apologies. Everybody was honest and genuine.

Those were days when with many people at the table we might have 11 kinds of potato salad, because we were all too poor to buy wieners. Everyone brought food. I wonder if A.A.s today appreciate how pitifully poor most of us were in those early struggling days.

It makes me sick to attend some A.A. groups today—I've visited A.A.s from Ohio to California—and see the wives sitting together in a clique. They don't step out and meet the new ones.

Anne never forgot newcomers. She knew the wives needed hospitalization as much as the men. The alcoholic gets lots of attention—the man's sponsor takes care of that. The other wives should look after the newcomer wife.

Nowadays when many A.A.s are back on their feet again and are fairly prosperous, I am struck with the fact that at Christmas parties many A.A. women are gaily dressed. But the poor ones, the new ones, still too deep in debt to be nicely dressed, and with nothing to be gay about, they hang around the edges feeling cold and lonely and forgotten.

Anne Smith hated to wear a new dress. I remember one party we were all going to. I had my first new dress, the first bought since my husband had stayed sober long enough to hold down a decent job. I asked Anne which dress she was going to wear, because I knew she had two new ones.

She answered, "I hate to wear a new dress. So many people will be there who can't afford a new one. I hate to embarrass them."

It was this bigness of heart, this continual thinking of others besides herself, that enabled Anne to help shape a formless group into what was presently to become A.A.

I hope we never lose sight of Anne's use of religion in building her own life and rebuilding the lives of the fearful wrecks who looked to her for guidance and strength.

I hope we never forget her humility, her courage, her cheerfulness, her unsparing use of herself.

Anne made me realize that all my years of misery have been

of some account, because I have been able to translate them into
usefulness; into helpfulness for other people.

I have known women who, for instance, lost sons in the war,
and ever since then they live in the past, constantly bemoaning
their loss and curdling every life they come in contact with. Why
don't these lonesome and heartbroken women go and visit sick
boys in the veterans' hospitals and try to bring a little cheer into
the world?

Anne didn't harm other people because she had suffered.
Rather, her life was rich because she was able to help people.

Anne never stopped living. She went on to reach out and
touch other lives.

I think of her every time I hear that familiar but little under-
stood verse: "He that loseth his life shall save it." Anne lost herself
in her work for A.A. Thereby she gained a new and bigger life.

A Cleveland minister in writing about A.A. summed things
up in this sentence: "Freedom is the ability to get outside yourself
and lose yourself in the thoughts and activities of others." That's
what Anne did.

——Dorothy

I WOULD LIKE TO ADD that I had the opportunity on several occasions to spend time with Ruth G., one of the AA wives whose letter
is included above. We visited in 1988 at her Adrian, Michigan, home.
I recall our first visit. After a brief introduction, Ruth looked at me
and said, "We came into AA in Dr. Bob and Anne's home on Ardmore
Avenue."

At that time, having had no prior information, I responded, "Oh,
so you're in AA." She smiled and said, "No, but back then we were
all welcome." Ruth told me that her husband, Ernie, was AA member
number seventy-eight and that he sobered up in May 1939 just after
the Big Book, *Alcoholics Anonymous,* was published.

Ruth was a delightful person who loved to talk. When I met her
for the first time, she was the picture of what I thought Anne must
have looked like. She was wearing a long dress with her hair up—very

proper—and she offered me a cup of tea. We sat and talked for a while; she was very excited to tell me about meetings at both the Smiths' home and that of T. Henry and Clarace Willliams in Akron. She loved to tell of how welcoming Anne was and how comfortable Ruth was with her. At the end of that first visit, Ruth said, "Please come back anytime."

I agreed that I would, and we set a date for the following Friday. When I returned to her apartment on the appointed day, Ruth was waiting for me. She had typed up small cards with affirmations on them to share with me. Each time I came after that she had additional cards to give me, as well as handcrafted crosses she had made just for me.

Ruth loved to entertain me with stories of Oxford Group meetings and the early AA members. Her recollections were of both the husband and his wife being considered members of the AA group. She often talked of how important the developing fellowship was to both Ernie and her—stressing that they were all trying to live by spiritual principles.

I listened to her reminisce about picnics, parties, and camping trips to Minnesota. She told me that she and Ernie would share a cabin with Dr. Bob and Anne. They would fish, cook, and play cards. I could tell that she dearly missed those days but was also very grateful for them. The conversations often turned toward Anne and how she influenced all of them with her spiritual practices. Had I known back then that I would later be writing about these experiences, I would have probed much deeper. Nevertheless, my life has been enriched by this relationship.

Ruth attended open AA meetings with her husband until his death in the early 1980s. She was influenced strongly by the Oxford Group and the teachings she learned while attending the group's meetings. She discussed the "Four Absolutes" (honesty, purity, unselfishness, and love) with me, explaining that she and her husband had attempted to live by these principles. She talked of surrender and confession and following God's guidance in all aspects of living.

I don't recall if Ruth ever joined Al-Anon Family Groups, but she participated in meetings with the wives for many years and continued to support and encourage everyone she met. I'm certain she would tell me that this is exactly how Anne S. lived her life.

There seems to have been one underlying theme to the life of Anne Smith and that was *love*. Love for God and her fellows. She worked tirelessly with many alcoholics, their wives, and families. Her life was an example of faith at work. Incidentally, her favorite Bible verse was James 2:26: "For as the body without the spirit is dead, so faith without works is dead also."

Because Anne stayed in the background and did her work quietly, there is only one known recording of her voice. The recording was made in her bedroom in June 1947. Anne, Dr. Bob, Bob Jr., and Betty each recorded a brief message, which was then delivered to Bill and Lois W. Their voices were recorded on a "wire," which is now part of my archives. The following is Anne's message to Bill and Lois:

> *Robert wants me to start first. He's afraid. We've got Betty and Bob Jr. here with us and George H. We are all up in my bedroom where we entertain now—it's very formal entertaining now as you can imagine. It's very nice of you to invite both Bob and myself down to Bedford Hills and we'd love to come. But, at present, I imagine we will have to stay put at 855 Ardmore. This is a new experience for me. I had a moving picture taken of myself and now I'm recording, so you see even with a bum eye I'm alive and kicking. Here's Robert.*[11]

It's easy to see from the stories about Anne shared by those who knew her how she influenced both the AA program and the wives' groups, which later became the Al-Anon Family Groups. Quite possibly, if Anne S. had lived a few years longer, she would have been considered a cofounder of Al-Anon.

Nevertheless, her work continues to grow today in meeting halls and at kitchen tables all over the world. Each time a suffering alcoholic is presented with the spiritual solution through the Twelve Steps and finds the loving embrace of the fellowship of Al-Anon or AA, Anne's spirit is present.

She knew that all hurting people needed and deserved love and understanding. Her example of continued fellowship, love, and kindness may be her most important contribution to the entire

Twelve Step movement. Wouldn't the world be a better place if each one of us could adopt more of her philosophy?

In the July 1949 *AA Grapevine,* Bill Wilson said this about Anne:

> *Her wise and beautiful counsel to all, her insistence that the spiritual come before anything else, her unwavering support of Dr. Bob in all his works—all these were virtues which watered the uncertain seed that was to become A.A. Who but God could assess such a contribution? We can only say that it was priceless and magnificent. In the full sense of the word, she was one of the founders of Alcoholics Anonymous.*[12]

Anne S. dedicated her life to serving others, to helping families, and to encouraging individuals to build their relationships with each other and with God. She was truly loved by everyone who knew her. The support she gave Dr. Bob was only a small illustration of Anne's character. When Dr. Bob made his farewell talk at AA's First International Convention held just one year after Anne's death, he said, "Our 12 Steps, when simmered down to the last, resolve themselves into the words 'LOVE AND SERVICE.'"[13] There are no words that better describe the life of Anne S.

In her book *Lois Remembers,* Lois Wilson said: "Annie's part in the formation of AA and consequently in the foundation of Al-Anon should never be forgotten, especially by family group members. Although there were few family groups during the thirteen years of her activity, Annie did much to instill the spirit of Al-Anon in many of the families of alcoholics. God bless Annie's memory."[14]

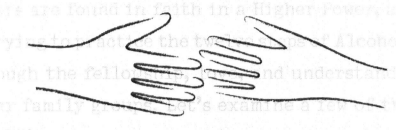

TWO

The Traveler: Myrtle L.

During the 1940s, "family groups" began to form in cities throughout the United States and Canada. Most of these early groups were made up of AA wives. As time went on, some husbands, fathers, and mothers of alcoholics also began to get interested. The groups used different names such as NAA (Non-Alcoholics Anonymous) and AAA or Triple A (Alcoholics Anonymous Auxiliary) until the founding of Clearing House in 1951. Clearing House became "Al-Anon Family Groups."

The July 1950 *AA Grapevine* stated: "According to the Foundation records the first non-alcoholic group started in Long Beach, California, on March 1, 1945. Since then groups have sprung up in Texas, Virginia, Michigan, upper New York State, and in Canada. There are probably others but, as this issue goes to press, these are the only ones actually heard from."[1]

One of the early auxiliary members was Myrtle L. from Colorado

City, Texas. Myrtle loved to travel and did so extensively during her years in NAA and subsequent years in Al-Anon. Myrtle's story exemplifies both the struggles of the original family groups and the hope these incredible people found once they banded together. As she tells her story, she makes many references to being an AA. Although non-alcoholic, she and the other wives considered themselves part of AA because they found their strength in the AA program.

As retold here, this account is adapted from three recordings and several letters in the Recovery Speakers Library archives.

·············

It's a well-established fact that there are no authorities in Alcoholics Anonymous so I don't presume to set myself up as any authority or to give any advice as to what you should or should not do. It's only out of a deep sense of gratitude for what the family groups of AA have given me that I share my story with you.

Then again, I realize that it's only as we contribute that we become part of something bigger. In some places today, although not nearly as many as there used to be, members of AA feel that the program of Alcoholics Anonymous is for members only and the family has no part in the program whatsoever. Therefore, our early groups decided to work very quietly, not interfering with AA in any way but striving to develop our own character, hoping that our actions might prove that this program is a way of life for anyone, regardless of the problem. Our goal was to become part of the cure instead of part of the disease.

Thank God for Anne S. and Lois and all those early wives who stuck! They made it possible for you, me, and thousands of others who by sharing our experience, strength, and hope can find peace and serenity in this way of life.

I'm an ordinary wife of a typical alcoholic—if there is such a thing as a typical alcoholic. I've been part of the disease and I'd like to be part of the cure. I know that my cure is people— those who have had the same grief and worries that I have had. The answers are found in faith in a Higher Power, and in working and trying to practice the Twelve Steps of Alcoholics Anonymous through the fellowship, love, and understanding that we find in our family groups.

Let's examine a few of these things. First, alcoholism is not my problem except as a by-product. My own defeated life and its reconstruction is the real problem I have to deal with. Since becoming involved with AA and the family groups in 1949, I've had some very wonderful experiences, some funny ones, and some tragic ones, and I've made an awful lot of stupid blunders.

The need for sobriety in our home was so great and so obvious that it tended to overshadow everything else. Sometimes it comes as quite a shock that sobriety alone is not enough. Sobriety without contentment, to me at least, is worthless. And to gain contentment we have to learn how to live. A lot more is needed than just the absence of alcohol. Anyone who has ever loved an alcoholic, anyone who has had to helplessly stand by for years watching the vicious progress of this disease is bound to develop fears and bound to develop frustrations. We need help—we've suffered with them.

Sometimes we lose our personal and financial security not once, but time and time again. Many of us had to assume responsibility; we became mother, nurse, and warden of very bad boys. So once there is an absence of alcohol in our homes, we also need to adjust to a new program of thinking; we need a fresh outlook on life. The AA [Al-Anon Family Group] program is successful because it offers just that. The question is, do we want it? And if so, are we willing to do anything about it?

The only story I have to tell you is my own and I don't intend to glue you to your seats while I grind out a long sordid tale. I'd much rather tell you about some of the things that I've learned and some of the things that have meant something to me.

My childhood wasn't happy. I was raised in church and I loved the music and the social end of it but the teachings were just words. I was so busy living that I didn't have a philosophy of life. I believed in God but had no faith. I thought that any problem could be solved by reason and common sense. While still quite young, I married an alcoholic. I knew nothing about alcoholism. After eight years of marriage he was accidentally killed, leaving me with two small daughters.

At that time I started my nursing career in our small town hospital. Three years later, in the middle of the Depression, the hospital temporarily closed its doors and I married another alcoholic. I knew he drank on occasion, but he was different. He was a hard worker and a happy drinker. He loved me, he loved my children, and he just loved everybody. So there wasn't too much of a problem—at least not that we recognized for about the first fifteen years. Then for the next two or three years the progression was insidious and I discovered that I was involved in yet another situation that I couldn't change no matter how much effort or reasoning I put into it.

I rapidly grew into what I call a "Four D Adult." The four D's in my case were disillusioned, disappointed, later disgusted, and then finally full of despair. My thinking became so distorted that my whole life was overwhelmed and ruled by fear.

When the phone rang or I'd hear an ambulance siren, I would die just a little until I found out it wasn't my husband. Drinking was costing us too much and I don't mean just money. It was costing us everything! We couldn't get up in the morning and be civil to each other. We had constant arguments and hardly had a happy moment in our home. I tried everything to get him to stop: I drank with him, but he liked it. I didn't, it made me sick. I pleaded and coaxed, threatened and argued all to no avail. My husband kept drinking. I had reasoned it all out and knew that all he had to do was say no and quit.

Unfortunately and unbeknownst to me, he was an alcoholic. He had already passed that invisible line into alcoholism and he couldn't quit. He needed treatment but we didn't know what. All of the seemingly ordinary events in our lives were being magnified by fear that developed into real and imaginary emotional crisis. Everyone who has lived with alcoholism knows exactly what I mean.

I spent my life wound up with fear or worry of one sort or another. I was afraid of debt, gossip, and disgrace. I was afraid of people; my fear was so deep I would cross the street to avoid talking with someone. I was afraid someone might ask me questions and I didn't want anybody to know what was going on in our home. I didn't have answers and I was ashamed. I was left with no hope, no faith, and I was sick.

With my father's help we moved north of town. The last two years of lone drinking were horrible. I worked at the hospital and wept. One day his old drinking buddy came by the hospital on business and I told him about my husband. He went out and talked to my husband, which was enough to get him to stop drinking and go to AA.

He stayed sober about ten months, and then went on the binge of all binges. He eventually got so bad he suffered with DTs. To cut a long nightmare short, he finally came out of it and started back to AA.

I thought, "Surely this is it! Our troubles are all over. He's sober now and back in AA." What a sad awakening it was to recognize all of the other maladjustments and character defects we had both developed. His sobriety was so important to me that I was going to try my best to help him "get" the program. This was the biggest blunder of my life.

Let me explain it this way: during the prolonged siege of alcoholism, a very curious phenomenon takes place in the relationship between an alcoholic and his wife. She is not only his wife; she becomes his mother as well. I thought that pressure of some sort was absolutely essential to his success in or out of AA. Let's say I had an overdeveloped sense of responsibility about his sobriety. Most of us learn the hard way that it can't be done this way in AA.

We can be helpful, but not when it comes to working his

program for him. This requires the individual's effort. No one can get the program or work the program for someone else. We have to get our program our own way. I believe we must develop a philosophy of living according to our own individual needs and we should ask questions and get the answers in our own good time. Nobody else can do this for us; I call this "hands off."

As I mentioned, I had a belief in God but I wasn't using it. I also believed in evil and have discovered that "fear" comes from having more belief in evil than in God. To me, there is a big difference between a belief and faith. A belief is in my head. Faith is in my heart and in my hands. I'm aware of a belief, but I live by faith.

I had also heard a lot about prayer and wondered why it hadn't worked for me. I began to realize that those who prayed successfully were humble people. They prayed for guidance and to be shown how to solve their own problems in God's way. I had pictured God as my handyman who should give me all the answers, my way—right now. It had never occurred to me that my way might not be God's way for me, and now might not be the time.

One night I was sitting in a meeting and I noticed the slogan "But for the grace of God." I was intrigued and later I looked up the word "grace." It was defined as a "gift" freely given, expecting nothing in return—a loving care. This appealed to me. I liked it, so I decided to try to turn my alcoholic over to this loving care and stop worrying about him. It freed me to do something about my own problems with God's help and the family group fellowship. It works! That is when I learned "IF I'M GONNA PRAY, WHY WORRY? IF I'M GONNA WORRY, WHY PRAY?"

When I stopped to think about it, I realized that God had been taking care of him all these years. Who else but God could have kept him alive and out of serious trouble all those drinking years? All I had to do was to "let go."

As time went on and he stayed dry, things became even more

baffling than they were while he was drinking and I found myself discouraged and in a worse rut than ever. I began to question, "Where is this peace of mind, this serenity? I haven't got it." I've heard it said that "our thoughts are the tools with which we mold our character and our lives." With the sort of thinking I had been doing I was molding a moldy sort of life for myself.

A speaker once said that positive thoughts are "builder uppers" and negative ones are "tearer downers." I recognized that over a period of years I had built a habit of thinking that was all negative. Habits are difficult to break and they were slowly controlling me. When I came to the Family Groups and found hope, I thought I had automatically reprogrammed my thinking, but I had not. I had only exchanged my past negative, fearful thoughts for a new set of negative, controlling, self-centered ones. I still had fears, they were just different ones. I had "Stinking thinking," which had paralyzed my usefulness and, finally, just like the alcoholic who realizes he has hit bottom, I had hit bottom.

This brought me to the realization that I needed help and I needed it for myself. This time I needed it badly enough to do something about it. At this point, just as the alcoholics do, I had some decisions to make for myself. First of all, could I be honest with myself and stop justifying all my deficiencies by blaming them on the situations around me? Was I willing to accept criticism with an open mind? Was I willing to get down off the pedestal I had been on for so many years and become teachable for a change? Could I keep an open mind and see my part in things? (This is a touchy one!) Could I learn to pray "giving" instead of "getting"? And, finally, was I ready to start now?

The Steps are the tools by which I've learned to live with reasonable contentment and balance in my life. Let me share just a little of my experience with the Steps.

Step One—"We admitted we were powerless over alcohol—that our lives had become unmanageable." If my life had been manageable, why hadn't I been able to manage being happy? If I wasn't happy about the situation around me, why didn't I change it? I couldn't; therefore my life was unmanageable.

Step Two—*"Came to believe that a Power greater than myself could restore me to sanity."* I didn't like the word "sanity." It was alright for the alcoholics to say that they were a little on the wacky side, but I didn't think that word applied to me. As I started getting a little more honest, I looked up the word "sanity." One definition I read said "Sanity: a healthy state of mind." Well, that was good enough for me. How could a mind as full of negative thoughts, fears, anxiety, and frustrations as mine be a healthy mind? So the doubts vanished and I could see that I needed to be restored.

Step Three—*"Made a decision to turn our will and our lives over to the care of God* as we understood Him." If He could do such a good job with thousands of hopeless drunks, He could do it for me too—if I'd just get out of the driver's seat and let Him take over.

Step Four—*"Made a searching and fearless moral inventory of ourselves."* This is a Step I didn't particularly like doing. To me, it was not so much a list of the things I have done, but things that I am and have become. This takes a lot of courage and honesty and I didn't have too much of either. But it was a starting point.

Step Five—*"Admitted to God, to ourselves, and to another human being the exact nature of our wrongs."* Facing my mistakes and admitting them to myself seemed relatively easy. It wasn't so difficult to admit them to God, either. I figured if He was going to steer the boat He might as well know there were some holes in the bottom of it. But this business of sharing with another person was a tough one for me. However, as I worked through these things, I began to get a wonderful sense of release and freedom.

Step Six—*"Were entirely ready to have God remove all these defects of character."* This meant I must be "entirely ready" to give them up, not just until I had an excuse to use them again. I must be ready to get rid of them—recognizing that these things are blocking my way to happiness and they're things I'm better off without. I trust God to do the job; I just need to get out of the way.

Step Seven—*"Humbly asked Him to remove our shortcomings."* It was "news to me" that I should be humble and admit that somebody else could do something better than I could for a change. It's my job to believe that He will, and it's my job to see to it these don't come creeping back again.

Step Eight—*"Made a list of all persons we had harmed, and became willing to make amends to them all."* Right at the top of the list of people I needed to make amends to, was me. I couldn't make any progress whatsoever in this program with remorse for the mistakes I had made in the past riding on my shoulders. Many of these mistakes were made through ignorance; but, nevertheless, they were mistakes and I was sorry for them.

Step Nine—*"Made direct amends to such people wherever possible, except when to do so would injure them or others."* Now the best way that I can do this is to find a new way of living and to make a conscientious effort to do something right. I can best make amends to my alcoholic husband by forgetting the past. You can't forgive if you can't forget! I had to learn to train my "forgetter," just like I had [to train] my memory. I could do it; I just had to do this in reverse. There were plenty more amends to make to my family and others and some of these took time.

Step Ten—*"Continued to take personal inventory and when we were wrong promptly admitted it."* To me this is the "daily dust up." It's a lot easier to keep things clean than it is to clean them up when they get good and dirty. "Promptness" is a good word to put in the Step because, when I put it off, I start to justify things again and sometimes I'm not so willing to admit that I was wrong.

Step Eleven—*"Sought through prayer and meditation to improve our conscious contact with God, as we understood Him, praying only for knowledge of His will for us and the power to carry that out."* This Step is my pet of them all. This is "First things first" and "Thy will be done, not mine." I'm asking for the ability to do the job as God sees it, not as I see it, and sometimes that is a very, very different thing.

Step Twelve—*"Having had a spiritual awakening as the result of these steps, we tried to carry this message to alcoholics, and to practice these principles in all our affairs."* At last I am awake to what life really can mean. I was half dead for years and the old shell was broken, and now I'm hatching out.

Looking back, I can see that the one decision I made which started me on a program of recovery for myself was, "I am no longer trying to help my alcoholic with his AA program or whatever program he might have for living." This one decision allowed me to break the shackles of alcoholism, which freed me to get started on a program of living for myself. I've learned that there is only one person I'm sure to live with all the rest of my life and it's me. It now seems sensible to make that person into the kind of person I'm going to enjoy living with.

The Al-Anon Family Groups have been an inspiration to me. Without them I may have gotten a start, but I seriously doubt it. It's been in the family groups that we get together, study our own program, and have our own discussions—here we tackle things from the non-alcoholic perspective. If we put a little in, we get a little out. If we put a lot in, we get a lot out. We try to stay pretty close to the Twelve Steps and the Twelve Traditions.

Every twenty-four hours gets better than the last—today's the day! I'm enjoying today; this is the one I've been waiting for! This is the only day I have so why don't I take the faith I have today and the abilities I have today and live it, giving thanks for it. I know what I want out of life; do you know what you want? I know exactly what I want now; I want whatever my Higher Power thinks I should have.

I want the courage to remember to try! I never know what I'm going to be able to do until I try. No matter how many failures I've had, this is another day. Perhaps I have more ability today; perhaps there are more opportunities today. This may be it, the day I have been waiting for. I want to meet each day with a good, strong, solid faith; and with God's help, I can make any day a good day, if I keep it well lived, well shared, and well appreciated. ⌐o

AS YOU CAN SEE from Myrtle's story, she maintained an exceptional attitude and worked continuously to develop her faith. Many of the letters, fliers, programs, and transcriptions I have in my personal archive from the 1950s originally were donated by Myrtle to the Midwest Tape Library. She was a frequent visitor to Montreal, New York, and Toronto. The following notes, edited here, were written after she had attended an AA conference in Toronto the last weekend in March 1953. The guest AA speaker was Bill D.—AA number three. Bill D.'s wife, Henrietta D., attended the conference with him, and, just as he was the third AA member, Henrietta was the third Family Group member.

After the morning panel, which ten wives attended, Myrtle joined others for a banquet lunch. From her letter dated March 28, 1953:

. . . .

I sat at the banquet table, informally, next to Henrietta D. I visited with her awhile before I discovered she was the wife of the third AA, Bill D., from Akron. Rather than go to the 1:30 panel, she and I sat in the corner with Annie S. (the Rock of Gibraltar) and had a wonderful informal discussion. We listened to Henrietta talk about the birth of AA. She and Bill, a lawyer, had a son. They both worshiped, but Bill drank up nearly everything so they couldn't even dress nor do things for their son decently. She attended church regularly and prayed always (to no avail) but was full of self-pity and resentment.

One day she had been to a P.T.A. meeting and Bill arrived home first, and was staggering around the front yard. She picked up a child's broom and hit him over the head with it. He just looked at her and said, "That is what you ought to have done." Bill was never abusive.

He had been in a private hospital several times until they refused him entrance because on previous visits he had run up and down the halls naked. He needed to be restrained and they didn't do that. Their family doctor (who was trying to protect Bill's reputation since he was a prominent lawyer) took him to another hospital. They tied him down beautifully there.

On his last trip to the hospital, his doctor was out of town and Henrietta didn't want to call another doctor. She was finally told to bring him on in to the emergency room and they would figure out something. Just as he was brought in, Dr. Bob called to see if they had a drunk he and Bill W. could "work on." So, they called on Bill D. as you read in the Big Book!

Even this early they stressed that the patient must surrender to God, and they kept him there until he did. Henrietta said he had nothing to eat but sauerkraut and tomato juice for eight days. She went to the hospital one day and Bill D. was crying, which was very unusual. Henrietta phoned Dr. Bob about it. Dr. Bob called Bill W. and said, "Come on over, Bill is crying; now is the time." Apparently it was; then and there he obviously had a spiritual awakening and never drank again.

Dr. Bob, Bill, and Anne went out to Henrietta and Bill's home every night for about two months. They always read and discussed the Bible. The book of James was their favorite. Anne phoned several times a day to see how things were going.

Bill W. got to talking religion with Henrietta. She assured him that she was a Christian; she attended church regularly and didn't dance, drink, or smoke. (She smokes now.) She always prayed and didn't have any sins. Bill asked her if she didn't feel a lot of self-pity, resentment, and bitterness about what alcohol had done to her and her son. She admitted that she did and he showed her that those were sins. He asked her to get down on her knees with him and Anne and pray, which she did. Henrietta said she remembered that after they had finished she didn't feel any different, but during the night she woke up and felt a beautiful glow all inside her. She knew instantly that everything was going to be all right and that her husband, Bill, would never drink again. She said she knew it! She is a lovely, shy person, very humble and serene.[2] ⌐o

MYRTLE WAS INVITED to speak at many AA and Al-Anon events around the country. She was a guest speaker at the 1955 AA International Convention in St. Louis. There is little doubt that she helped many people throughout her journey to find serenity and peace, just as she had found them. Her ability to communicate the principles contained in the Twelve Steps and her willingness to share them with others illustrate her dedication to service. Her legacy lives on because she accepted "grace" or, as she liked to call it, "the gift."

When sharing Myrtle's story, I would be thrilled to say that everything worked out wonderfully in her life. However, while she continued on through the years as an active member of Al-Anon—dealing with life on life's terms—her husband, unfortunately, continued to struggle with his sobriety. Even after his death, the family was tormented by his alcoholism. In a letter from 1976, Myrtle shared the following: "I wonder if all the stigma of the disease of alcoholism will ever be erased. Maybe in later generations! I had a horrible taste of that when at my husband's funeral the preacher talked about his alcoholism and apparently couldn't find a place to stop! I didn't know or dream he would do it."[3]

She went on in this letter to discuss some serious problems this incident created for her with other family members. I could tell from the tone of the letter that Myrtle was able to forgive the preacher for his ignorance and lack of understanding. I'm sure she continued to pray that one day, society as a whole would understand that alcoholism is an illness and that the stigma would vanish. She clearly understood that both the alcoholics and their families are not bad people needing to get good, but sick people needing to get well.

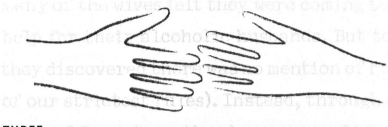

THREE

Sound Homes: The First International Convention of AA

n July 1950, Alcoholics Anonymous held its First International Convention in Cleveland, Ohio. Every five years since then, AA has done likewise with the most recent convention, as of this writing, held in the summer of 2010 in San Antonio, Texas.

This first convention marked some of AA's most important events to date: Dr. Bob Smith delivered his farewell message, the AA Traditions were accepted by the fellowship, and the non-alcoholic wives held their first major meeting with no AA involvement.

This "non-alcoholic" meeting was very successful and clearly showed that the non-alcoholics had developed a program that was separate from the AA fellowship, but that used the same successful principles. Lois W. kicked off the meeting and then turned things over to a group of women from Toronto. The contents of these speeches were recently located after having been lost for sixty years: the talks by Lois W., Pearl E., and Edith B. were found on a reel-to-reel tape, and the others were transcribed by Myrtle L. and donated to the Midwest Tape Library. Included here are the full transcriptions of this historic event, starting with Lois W.'s brief introduction.

INTRODUCTION
Lois W.

The interest in the Family Groups has grown tremendously and some very fine non-alcoholic Family Groups have begun all over the country. One of the very finest, in fact, is in Toronto and we have with us a team of women who have come down from Toronto and are going to talk to us this evening. Their chairman is Pearl, and I will ask her to take over the meeting.[1]

"SOUND HOMES THROUGH WIVES" APPROACH TO AA
Chairman – Pearl E., Toronto

We welcome you all most heartily to this meeting, and it is with great pleasure. And I may say with great humility, that the speakers on this panel—representing the Wives' Groups of Toronto—will endeavor to tell you something of the program we have attempted to follow. I have been requested to tell you something of the history of our Wives' Group.

Having had such a tremendous victory over the problem of alcohol in our own home, naturally, I was anxious to pass this joy and happiness on to other wives of alcoholics. But realizing my inadequacy for this great challenge, and not knowing any wife of an alcoholic to help, I called on a friend who had been of great help to me—but who had had no experience of alcohol. She agreed to help me, knowing the answer is the same to any problem.

After much earnest consideration, a Wives' Group was formed, a few months after AA was founded in Toronto, Canada, in 1943, seven years ago. Six or seven wives met in our home every two weeks. This effort was not without opposition. As in most places today, many of the AA members felt this program was for alcoholics only—that the wives had no part in the program whatever. So it was decided we should work very quietly, not interfering with AA members in any way, but striving to develop our own character; hoping our actions might prove this program is a constructive way of life for anyone, regardless of our problem. [We hoped] that we might become part of the cure, instead of part of the disease, as is the case in many homes; that by our attitude in the home we might promote a spirit of cooperation, whereby the family could work this program out together.

In first attending meetings, many of the wives felt they were coming to a meeting to find some help for their alcoholic husbands. But to their great surprise, they discovered there was no mention of husbands (this being one of our strictest rules). Instead, through studying the Fourth Step Moral Inventory, they began to realize some of their own faults. Then they began to wonder, if, after all, their honest desire in having the husband stop drinking was not more for their own comfort, rather than the alcoholic's recovery.

As we studied this program and came to see and know ourselves, we did change and our husbands noticed this change and they, too, began to realize the still greater miracle of this AA way of life. Many homes were changed; they became sound homes, where joy and happiness took the place of fault-finding and nagging. They were healthy homes where no delinquency could develop and where children could find their rightful heritage, through an atmosphere of peace and love.

Soon, we grew too big for one home. Then we branched out to another group and still another, until today we have six groups for wives of AA in Toronto, with one in each corner of the city.

Now we hope the out-of-town groups may see fit to follow, and find through their AA groups the joy and happiness that we have found and that you are going to hear about today.

I have much pleasure in calling on our first speaker, Edith B. Edie is going to tell you what teamwork in the home has meant to her family. She is the mother of two small children and has been associated with our Wives' Group for four and a half years.

Our next speaker is Anne. She will tell you how she has found personal serenity. Though the alcoholic problem in her home is still unsolved, she has found peace of mind in spite of her problem. She has been associated with our Wives' Group for two years.

Anna A. is our next speaker. Anna has two children. She is learning to establish harmony and unity in her home, through her practice of the spiritual program of AA. Anna has been associated with our Wives' Groups for three years.

Our last speaker is Ione G. She will tell you about the miracle of AA and how it works in her own home. Ione is the mother of two grown-ups, a son and a daughter. She is also a grandmother. Ione has been associated with Wives' Group for three and a half years.

After hearing our speakers today, I am sure you will realize the tremendous part a wife can play through practicing this AA program. And I do appeal to you as wives and mothers to recognize your great responsibility. I would also ask you to remember, "Sound Homes," united homes, mean sound nations and sound nations mean peace—which we all want and which is the answer to our nation's need today.[2]

TEAMWORK IN THE HOME
Edith B., Toronto

It is a well-established fact that there are no authorities in Alcoholics Anonymous. We, who are speaking today, don't presume to set ourselves up as any authority or to give advice to anyone as to what they should or should not do. We will try to express the happiness and contentment which we have gained through our association with AA. And we would like to tell you how this has been achieved through the process of trial and error.

In our discussion of teamwork in AA, we are using the term in reference to the alcoholic and his or her non-alcoholic mate working together, in harmony, toward a mutual goal. This idea of teamwork is not new by any means. Bill, the founder of AA, and his wife, Lois, have been cooperating in this work from the very beginning. But new or not, it is pretty wonderful to us.

You see, nearly every married couple that comes to AA represents a marriage that has been virtually shattered by alcoholism. Our marriages were originally based on love and trust and mutual understanding, but over a period of years, as the alcoholic problem increased, these were replaced by disgust, disillusionment, confusion, and bitterness. Those of us who did survive legal separation were held together by very frail threads. In my own case, we were held by a small hope, a large fear, and two children.

We came to AA together because we were both frightened of the future, and tired of fighting against something we knew nothing about. Some years before this, I came to realize that my husband drank because he had to, not because he wanted to. He was compelled and driven by some strange obsession, entirely beyond his will. At this time, there was very little known about the disease of alcoholism and we knew absolutely nothing. For years, we worked together, trying to find some way of controlling it, but despite our desperate efforts, it defeated us at every turn. Our mutual decision to turn to AA was just one more step in the dark, and, frankly, we had gone about as far as we could go.

We came, like so many others, for just one thing—sobriety for the alcoholic—thinking that if he were sober, we could readjust our lives and be completely happy. He learned that sobriety without contentment was nothing, and to gain the contentment, he had to learn how to live. Well, I had to live with him, so I thought I'd better learn, too.

We attended meetings together and thank God nearly all our meetings are open meetings and we non-alcoholics are welcome. We listened to the speakers, discussed the literature, and gradually began to get a little understanding of AA and a great deal of enthusiasm for more.

Right there, is where I made a big mistake that I hope others will avoid. I ignored the slogan "Easy does it" and tried to go at this in a great hurry. If there was something here for us, I wanted to take it all in big gulps, predigest the whole program, and feed it back to my partner in simple, quick doses.

Now, you see, I had been included in every effort that we had made so far to control this alcoholism, and I wanted very badly to be included in this one. But I went at it the wrong way. My idea of cooperation was to rush him past the taverns and push him into AA—all the time trying to guide and control him, in the way I thought was right. Believe me; I couldn't have been more wrong, because that didn't even keep him sober. He had a "slip" and it was a dandy. Now mind you, I'm not saying that my behavior caused the slip because I know now that it didn't, but I do think that I caused a lot of confusion that could have been avoided.

Fortunately, however, one of the wiser wives stepped in here and gave me the best bit of advice to date. She said, "All you need is some confidence and faith—confidence in his success and faith in the program." She pointed out that if I had no confidence in my husband, how in the world could I expect him to have any? Well, that looked a bit difficult because I hadn't placed any confidence in him for years, and, as for having faith, I hadn't any faith in anything. I was too full of fear for any faith to get in. But I thought, "If that's what I need, then that's what I'll try to get."

The faith grew, steadily but surely, when I began to realize that hundreds of other alcoholics, many worse than my husband, had successfully gained sobriety through this program.

Well, he probably had lots of faults, but he certainly wasn't stupid—if they could get it, then so could he. This faith was strengthened when I saw real evidence that this program was guided by some Higher Power. I began to depend on this Higher Power to see him safely through each day, and for the first time in my life, I prayed, believing. Surprisingly, that dispelled all the fear and worry, because If you pray, why worry? And if you worry, why pray?

We found, also, that success with this program is a matter of individual effort, and the progress of each person depends entirely on the degree of effort, he or she puts into it. I found that I couldn't work his program for him, so I tried to take my hands off and let him make his own way with the help of the alcoholics and the guidance of his Higher Power.

That was fine. He started to change his thinking and his way of living and began to get some fun out of this; but what about me? I was still in the same old rut. So the wives suggested that I join their group and start my own program. For this suggestion, I'll be grateful for the rest of my life because it has made the rest of my life worth living.

There are many ways of beginning this, but I started in on the slogans. I said:

Easy does it. Don't try to do all your work in one day. You'll make yourself so tired and irritable that no one can live with you.

Keep an open mind. Live and let live. Drop that smug, self-satisfied, "I-know-best" attitude. I could be wrong.

First things first. Attend to things in the order of their importance. Sobriety comes first in our home and then everything else in order. Get your sense of values straight. Tidy up your cluttered mind.

But for the grace of God. Don't be so darned critical and intolerant. Count yourself again—you ain't so many, and but for the grace of God, you'd be a lot less.

Twenty-four-hour program. Let me live each day to its fullest extent. No yesterdays crowding in to steal part of it. Yesterday is a dead horse; the past is gone and can't be recalled. NO tomorrows to think of with dread and anxiety because tomorrow isn't here yet.

So it's just today—twenty-four hours of doing first things first, the easy way. It's the best nerve tonic in the world.

From the slogans, I moved on to try the Twelve Steps, and if any of you think that they look easy—I'll agree with you. They do look easy, for someone else to do, but trying them myself was a different matter. I had faith that the Higher Power would see my partner through, but it wasn't until I handed over my own life to my Higher Power that I began to progress. At the moment that I began to ask for guidance and work the program, my husband and I began to be a real team.

I don't believe, in a readjustment like ours, that a truly harmonious home life is possible, unless both partners are working the program, because happiness and harmony in our home comes through sharing and mutual understanding. My husband and I, as a team, began our sharing in a very small way—sharing ideas and working out our problems together. Each evening before retiring, we have formed the habit of holding our own little AA meeting. We have a pot of tea, review our day, discuss our progress, and swap ideas. Although these little meetings are short on speakers, they've been wonderfully helpful to us.

Very early in AA we discovered that we couldn't pull together unless we pulled in the same direction and the only way we could be sure of pulling in the right direction was to ask for guidance. So gradually, our Higher Power became a member of our team in sort of a three-way hitch. He takes the lead in all things and we follow.

Our path hasn't been all velvet since we started this new way of life. Plenty of problems have arisen and probably always will, but we have found that the answer to any problem can be found through the Twelve Steps and asking for guidance each day. When a really big issue is involved and there doesn't seem to be any answer, we just hand it over to God and know that it will be done, the right way, at the right time.

Each day brings a challenge and to us the greatest challenge is in sharing our AA with others. Happiness is a paradox—we have to give it to others [in order] to keep it ourselves.

This, of course, is only one way of gaining peace of mind and contentment through the AA program. There are many ways, probably just as successful as ours, but to us it is the only way because it works for us. We hope to continue working along, side by side, and sharing the load because this way, we are together again and we're not only living—we're loving it![3]

PERSONAL SERENITY THROUGH PRACTICING AA PRINCIPLES IN ALL MY AFFAIRS

Anne S., Toronto

If anyone had told me two years ago that I would be speaking from a public platform, I would have said that person had taken leave of his senses. And only out of a deep sense of gratitude for what the wives of AA have given me, am I speaking today. Then again, I realize it is only as we contribute that we become part of something bigger.

I am the wife of an alcoholic. When I first came into the wives' group, I used to say, "I am one of those whose problem has not been solved yet." It wasn't long before I learned to say, more correctly, "My alcoholic problem has not been solved," because I came to realize that my own defeated life was the real problem with which I had to deal.

I think nearly all wives who have to live with alcoholic husbands suffer from fear, loneliness, frustration, self-pity, resentment, and failure to live a normal home life. I experienced all of these, but the greatest enemy of all was resentment. It filled my whole world! It grew to be a monster that ate up all power to think constructively. It warped my judgment and paralyzed my usefulness. Life became a thing without purpose. I forgot appointments; I went blocks past my stops when on buses and streetcars. I looked at people when they talked to me without knowing a word they were saying, for my own problem filled my mind to the exclusion of all other interests.

When I look back two years, I realize I was not quite sane, and if nothing had happened to change the situation, I believe I would have eventually ended up in the ward of a mental institution somewhere. *I was spiritually sick.*

Now we know that all life's experiences are just the outer expression of inner thoughts. In more familiar words, "As a man thinketh in his heart, so is he." So you can see that with my negative attitude towards life there wasn't much chance of building up a constructive pattern of living.

But we often find God when things are the blackest. Alcoholics often tell us they had to reach an extremity of suffering or degradation before they were willing to ask help from a Higher Power. They say they had "reached bottom." I believe it is so with most of us. Our self-sufficiency stands between God and us and we have to get a severe jolt or feel we have reached the end of our tether, before we seek God's help. But we often hear it said that "man's extremity is God's opportunity." I knew if anyone was to help me, it had to be a Power greater than myself, and I believe it was a direct answer to prayer when a friend persuaded me to attend one of the AA wives' meetings.

Imagine my disappointment when not a word was said about how to deal with my alcoholic husband. I was shocked and still more resentful at the suggestion that I might need a reconditioning of my own thoughts and way of life.

The wonderful thing about this AA program is that it is based on cooperation. We share our gifts. It doesn't deal in theories but is heart to God and hand to man. The whole crux of the program is working it and applying it to fit our own individual need. In it, we find a new way of life.

Through gaining a better knowledge of this disease called alcoholism, I saw that of myself, I was powerless over my alcoholic husband. I made a decision to turn my problem over to God. These, of course, are the first two steps of the AA program. During these two years, in trying to practice AA principles in my affairs, I have found a peace of mind, a new joy in living, and a detachment from my problem, I never could have believed possible; and, yet, nothing has changed but my attitude. We have been told, "Be ye transformed by the renewing of your mind."

Prayer is the only thing that will successfully change character. This opens up a whole study on the art of practicing successful prayers. If all the selfish prayers in the world were answered, can you imagine the chaos that would result?! I used to wonder why my prayers were never answered. Now I know they were completely selfish ones, most of them for the gratification of my own desires—neither was I ready, spiritually, to have some of these prayers answered. How could I expect God to answer the prayers of a person filled with enmity, self-pity, and resentment? I must pray instead for knowledge of His will and the power to carry that out. True prayer is a way of life, and it is vital to serenity and happiness.

Only as we let go and let God can we hope to overcome wrong mental habits acquired over many years. But as we grow spiritually, we get a keener awareness of our defects of character. When negative thoughts come into our minds, we have to deliberately substitute other thoughts for them—a loving thought for one of enmity; a thought of praise for one of criticism; one of forgiveness for one of resentment. If we just get our minds off "getting" and put them into "being," we soon get the right answers.

Carrying over into today the bitterness and the blunders of yesterday kept me full of self-pity and resentment. But the working of this program on a 24-hour basis, with a daily quiet time for prayer and meditation, gives us a confidence and faith. A right relationship to God is the key to serenity, both personal and world.

I'd like to close with the words of the Twelfth Step, which expresses exactly how I feel after two years of association with the wives of AA.

Having had my heart warmed and my soul fed, by friendliness and love exhibited in this organization, it is my desire to carry this message to other wives, and to practice these principles in all my affairs.[4]

HARMONY AND UNITY IN OUR HOME
Anna A.

I would like to tell you as clearly as possible what I am learning through the AA philosophy. To me, it has been a spiritual experience, and while I am quite aware that I have only started on the road to understanding, I think I have learned sufficiently that I know I could never relinquish it or turn back. Our home was not a broken home literally, but it was certainly not a united home. Gradually, I realized that these conflicts within and without could not be resolved through the power of reason, but only through my being willing to have my own attitude and character measured by a set of principles, which up to that time I had at times completely, and always partially, ignored.

I will take the Twelve Steps and attempt to tell you what spiritual truths I am learning as a result of the study and contemplation of this program through our wives' groups.

Our first step reads, "Admitted we were powerless to help an alcoholic and that our own lives had become unmanageable." [Various versions of this Step were used by wives' groups before the organization was unified.] I learned that thoughts are things and as such can be binding or freeing according to the quality of the thought and the thinker. Thoughts of criticism, condemnation, fear, worry, anger, anxiety, bitterness, hate, or a sense of having failed, are all negative, and have a destructive and binding nature both to the thinker and the person the thoughts are directed to. Conversely, thoughts of love, goodwill, blessing, praise, kindness, etc., are constructive and freeing. My life had become unmanageable because it was bound by negative thoughts. Through our discussion groups I am becoming increasingly aware of the nature and importance of thought, and try to the best of my ability to replace a negative attitude with a constructive one the moment I recognize it.

Step two is: "Came to believe that a Power greater than ourselves could restore us to sanity." My interpretation of this is, "Could restore us to a sane way of living." To me, that Power is God. I had always believed in God, but I also believed in evil, and I learned that fear is the result of having more faith in evil than in God. So I realized that I must establish faith in the Power before it could work for me.

For many weeks, day after day, I repeated to myself, "God is the only Power in my life." And one day it was a revelation to me when I had the conviction that God *is* the only Power in my life. It has been amazing to me that so little faith could warrant some of the events which have taken place in my life since that time. So I learned the truth that it is as we are told, "According to your faith, be it unto you."

Step three: "Made a decision to turn our will and our lives over to the care of God *as we understand Him.*" I found it necessary to clarify my idea regarding the nature of God, and as I contemplated this I realized that just because I did not understand certain things didn't mean they were not necessarily so. Also, it was not the image I created of God which counted, but it was the effort put forth which was important. So I went right back to the beginning and established in my mind, without a doubt this time, that "In the beginning there was God." I reread my daughters' *Hurlbut's Story of the Bible,* this time with an open mind. It was an amazing experience to me because for the first time I realized that it is a history of mankind, and of each individual.

I read the children's version because the stories are told in sequence, true to the original narrative, and in a language I could understand. I came to believe and know that God always has been, is now, and always will be. It is our own idea of separation which creates the gulf, and results in our own confusion. It is what we continually take into our minds in meditation which is brought into manifestation in our lives. I realized through this study that I unconsciously and consciously thought a great deal about all the so-called evil in my own life, as well as in the world at large.

By making the decision to turn my life over to the care of God as I understand Him, I found a wonderful release, and through this release my mind was free to be disciplined as I will. I find this requires persistent practice day after day, but in making this decision I found a new and definite purpose to devote my life to, but at the same time I know that this involves a very definite responsibility on my part. I must be willing to give up any and every thought of a negative nature, any idea of getting even.

The greatest help in trying to overcome adverse thoughts, desires, and situations has come to me with the constant repetition, and with the knowledge of what it implies, of "Thy will be done." I learned from this that God's will is goodwill and can only bring good into our lives. This decision I make daily, and each day I pray for guidance and knowledge of His will, for humility, for strength, and for courage to follow through.

The next four steps I am taking together. Through the understanding I acquired from the first three steps, I was in a better position to take a moral and spiritual inventory. I interpreted step five to read, "The exact nature of my wrong thinking." In our groups, we have the opportunity of admitting our mistakes and finding out a great many more which we didn't realize were mistakes. I found I was a super-sensitive person who was controlled by circumstances, and the thoughts of those I associated with influenced me greatly. If they were down, so was I.

Not long ago I read that there are two words not known in the vocabulary of an atheist or a pessimist; they are "praise" and "bless." I was not an atheist, but it seems that from the very beginning we have a choice. I am acquiring an understanding of the great commandment, "Thou shalt love the Lord God with all you heart, mind, and soul, and your neighbor as yourself." First, love of God; second, love of neighbor; and third, love of yourself. I found I had to love myself properly; otherwise I was not capable of loving my neighbor. I must forgive myself as I forgive others, and must not indulge in self-condemnation, which is a different matter entirely from admitting our mistakes.

Steps eight and nine I will also take together. At first, I had difficulty in deciphering these, but with an understanding of the nature of thought I had to confess my thoughts would never have passed a test of purity. To make amends I have adopted the simple method of asking each person or persons I have thought of unkindly or resentfully for forgiveness, and where I cannot do it with sincerity I simply ask God to assist me in feeling forgiving. And I always have had that assistance arrive and I am once again freed, and I believe that the receiver of the blessing has benefitted as well.

Step ten: "Continued to take personal inventory, and when we were wrong promptly admitted it." Lately I have learned what to me is the most important lesson regarding this step. No matter what situation or problem presents itself I ask myself this question: "What is there to be learned from this?" Every experience has become a lesson to be learned and I find that "All things do work together for good."

Step eleven: "Sought through prayer and meditation to improve our conscious contact with God." To me this is the loveliest of all the steps. I am learning how to pray, and my faith has increased a thousandfold. I know that to be effective prayer needs only a little faith and a little knowledge of His will. That we pray shows some faith; that we pray calmly and trustingly shows more.

If then, we can go forth thankfully and show in our words, thoughts, and actions that we believe the answer is forthcoming, the answer will come. Perhaps a different answer than the one we had thought, but I believe it will prove a more satisfying one than any we might have sought for ourselves. If I do not get an answer, I am learning to trace it back to my own attitude; quite often I find that I do not give God a chance, I become unreceptive. I get in a hurry and go after something else. But I do come back to my principle and faith because I find I must. I cannot be happy without the consciousness of God in my life.

The rewards of trying to pattern my life according to this program have been quite wonderful. One of the great joys is being able to pass on to another who is travelling the weary road I once trod, a message of hope and faith with the sincere conviction that if these principles work for me they will work for anyone. This is known as our twelfth step and I have come to believe that I shall only retain what I have so fully received by being willing to pass this message on to others. For these blessings and opportunities, I shall be forever grateful. Thank you.[5]

HAPPY HOMES THROUGH THE MIRACLE OF AA

Ione G., Toronto

It is the greatest pleasure and privilege to be on this platform. I always welcome the opportunity to tell of the miracle that has happened to our home through AA.

Today in AA we hear a great deal about miracles. Now what does that word "miracle" mean? The dictionary tells us it is something supernatural, superhuman, and something we cannot do ourselves. Now that is what happened to us. We, my husband and I, had tried everything, and failed! Of ourselves we could do nothing about this alcoholic problem. Now what happens to a home like that? — Slow disintegration. The breakup of everything one holds dear.

Then the question arises, is it better to break up a home like that? Would it be better for the children? MY answer has always been, "No." To stand by my marriage vows "for better or for worse." And besides, I loved my husband in spite of this horrible change that was taking place.

For us, the miracle started when our son returned from overseas. He decided he could not live at home, or work for his father, as things were. That decision was the turning point for us. My husband realized the end of the road had come for him. And my prayers were answered; for he then went to AA, and step by step we started to work the program together. That was when the miracle-working power of God made it possible for us to rebuild our lives and our home into a sound and happy home.

To start building that kind of home, I have found two things to be very necessary. First, I had to admit that I was powerless to help an alcoholic. Second, I had to accept and acknowledge that a "Power" or "God" as I understood Him could help us.

When I did that, my whole attitude gradually changed. My greatest discovery was that alcoholism is a disease — not a form of selfish indulgence or a weakness of character. To me it is most important that we wives keep that fact before us constantly. For these people are sick people! When a person is ill, you don't blame them, leave or neglect them, or censure them. You lovingly help them and encourage them.

In this disease particularly, it is most important for the alcoholic to feel that "somebody cares." (That is the slogan of the wives' groups.)

Fears, frustrations, and worries are the wife's greatest problems. Now how do we overcome these? First, we recognize and accept our powerlessness and God's power. Second, by working and living this program to the best of our ability (for ourselves alone) and taking our hands off the other person. Third, we work on the 24-hour plan, forgetting the yesterdays, and not thinking of the tomorrows, living for each day alone. Fourth, we put something better into each day than the day before.

Then, too, the AA slogans help us wives a great deal in working our own program. "Easy does it." To me that means putting no time limit on how quickly the alcoholic works the program or how he works it, not to push or rush him. SO many wives think the minute the husband goes to AA the whole pattern of their lives should change, at once! Believe me it does not work that way. For we, too, have to apply this program to ourselves and change our own lives, just as much as the alcoholic.

"First things first" means the husband's sobriety must be the first concern of the wife and family.

"But for the grace of God." Have you ever thought what that means? It could so easily have been you or I that had been the victim of this disease. Also and most important, "But for the grace of God" we would not be in AA.

Now at this point, our personality change starts. First, it gradually becomes not "who is right" but "what is right." Second, as we go on working and living this way, we become more tolerant, more understanding, more patient, and soon we can disagree but not be disagreeable. What a difference! These two things alone change the whole atmosphere of the home. Paul [the apostle] says something about building little colonies of heaven. Can you see what that means? Sound homes! Happy homes!

They can make the pattern for the kind of world we want our children to grow up in. Our AA program contains all the ingredients that make us into the kind of people who can build that kind of home. We become constructive instead of destructive, helpful instead of helpless, purposeful instead of purposeless, hopeful instead of hopeless. I see this whole program as a way of life that changes our character and nature. Some say human nature cannot be changed. But our program proves it can. It shows us how. But it is up to us to do it. No use asking God or the Higher Power to help us, then sit back and wait for something to happen. It is the trying to work this program to the best of our ability that counts. Now, we wives here in Toronto are most fortunate in having so many groups of our own.

To me, it is as important for us to go to our meetings as it is for the alcoholic to go to his. It is the clinic, as it were, where we have the opportunity to get down to our basic needs—where we, through our own program, interpret our steps through our own experience. It deals with our own character change, never that of a husband, nor do we discuss our husbands. We are much too busy getting this philosophy to work for us. Our needs are as great as the alcoholic's.

We, too, are sick people—sick in mind, in spirit, and often in body. For many, these groups offer the first and only opportunity of contact with other women, who not only have and under-stand their problem, but have the answers in their own lives.

We wives all think we are alone, that no one else has such a problem and because of that—and the shame that has always been attached to alcoholism—our pride makes us put up pre-tenses, to protect our situation from the censure and criticisms of our friends, who would not understand. For the wife who goes to a meeting or two, then says there is not much there for her, I can only say this. If your husband's sobriety means any-thing real to you, then, not only is there something there for you to get, but there is something for you to give. For the new wife, there is nothing more heartening than to see the wives who have been working this program for sometime still going to meetings.

For it is natural to want to turn to someone you know, who has attained a certain amount of success, in working the pro-gram. For me, through my trying to work and live this way of life, and through our wives' groups, I am now *the proudest, happiest, and most grateful woman.*

Proud, because the man I love and married and thought I had lost has come back. Happy, because we are the pals we started out to be, and we have understanding and peace. Grateful, because together we have found a way of life through AA which is so worthwhile; and with God's help, we are going to keep it that way.

IS THAT NOT A MIRACLE?[6]

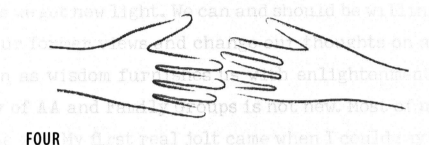

FOUR

Experience, Strength, and Hope

n the history of Alcoholics Anonymous, reference to the "flying blind period" is often made. Al-Anon, once organized, seemed to skip over this period and develop a solid foundation immediately. Certainly pre-Al-Anon, from 1936 to 1951, there were some groups that were "flying blind." However, many of the earliest Family Groups seemed able to learn from the mistakes made by AA or to simply avoid them with the use of exceptional judgment and wisdom.

At a Family Group panel held in Toronto in 1955, four early Canadian members shared their experiences in a session entitled "Keys to Better Understanding." Each woman spoke on one particular topic. The following is a transcription of their talks.

HOPE

Bertha M.

I came into Family Groups in self-defense—literally defense against myself. As a newcomer to Toronto, I found my life again changing and I was very lonely. "Hope" has been given me for my talk, as one of the "Keys to Better Understanding." Hope and family are such warm words—"hope," confidence in the future. "Family," as well as meaning wife, husband, and children, also means "a group with some common feature." We all have so much in common.

My experience in Family Groups is of only one year. That seems such a short time to undo what I had allowed to happen in my personality through misunderstanding of this problem.

Yet in humbleness I can say "time" can reconstruct very quickly if one is willing to accept the friendly help and understanding which is so much a part of "Family Groups." This I have proven in the past year. So being allowed to speak to you today is indeed a pleasure.

My story—for story it now has become, as it is in the yesterdays—follows a pattern so familiar to all wives of alcoholics. First, disbelief—it can happen to us—on to frustration, disillusionment, disappointment, and down to nagging and complete surrender to resentments.

My life today is so changed by the AA way of living that going back is only necessary when I find a smugness creeping in and my efforts lagging. Then a complete inventory is necessary and I find renewed "hope" in today, and yesterdays fall into just a story.

The pattern of my life before alcohol entered was of wholesome good living—never abundance of worldly goods, but where abundance of love and understanding was practiced. A home of religious training was practiced and, by example, made part of daily living. I was trained to stand on my own feet—trained to make decisions as wisely as possible, but not trained to combat the moral destruction caused by alcohol. So I was ill-prepared to cope with that.

An incident, very unimportant now, but years ago very important, happened the first Sunday in our own home. My husband went for a walk, met some pre-war friends, and the result was my first real experience in how drinking was to alter our lives.

Fear of what might be entered my very soul. I felt very much alone. Shame would not permit me telling anyone. For the first time in my life I could not take my problem to my parents. The first of many promises made and broken. I began then to build a wall of defense around myself. But resentment and fear replaced all hope in my thoughts.

So often our lives as wives, mothers, or sisters of alcoholics are seemingly "hopeless" through misunderstanding of this problem. Each time, "hope" seemed to wind up in despair and our defects of character came to the surface and erased all we knew was right. We wanted to be right but our interpretation of right at times became very warped. We, in our "helplessness" and "self-pity," tried to make our own laws of adjustment.

The position my husband held meant trips of several weeks duration. That started the many years of first protesting, then eventually nagging, and always such a fear of the future. This also meant loneliness and problems almost insurmountable to one alone. I tried to spare my children and really reached a very low ebb when I found I could not hide the alcoholic problem from them. I was truly defeated and turned to my father for advice. Even his kindly understanding and guidance could not arrest the bitterness I had allowed to alter my life. Utter "hopelessness" became so much a part of existence, with children entering their formative years, and I, a bitter, frustrated woman full of resentments and feelings bordering almost on hatred for what I was becoming. I remembered the good traits of character seemingly lost; I even doubted prayer—yet never completely lost my trust in God.

Then five years ago AA entered our lives.

I knew that for some unaccountable reason the period of not drinking was longer than usual—there had been many such good, happy periods, so full of hope. But they had not lasted too long. So I thought of this as just another one.

After several weeks I wanted to go to Rosemere, a small town outside Montreal, to see a very dear friend. I had been put off several times, so this evening I was determined to go and made an issue of no small proportions. Finally came the words that have been indelible in my mind ever since: "I cannot go. I have been going to Alcoholics Anonymous and this is our meeting night."

Words cannot describe what my thoughts were. Fear again—it couldn't be, after all these years—fear that I would cry—fear that I would laugh in disbelief. My only conscious thought, "Dear God, let it be so." Needless to say, we did not go to Rosemere.

As time went on, I dared not hope, for fear of being disillusioned again. We two were now alone. Loneliness, such as I had never known so deeply before, entered my life. I had played second fiddle to alcohol for many years. Now I was playing second fiddle to Alcoholics Anonymous, resenting that some stranger could have more influence in my husband's life than the children and I together.

We were not so fortunate in Montreal in open meetings, so for two years I was not included. I knew my husband had something he needed and that seemed sufficient for a good way of living. I seemed to need so much, but was not ready to admit my need.

So what then to do; I tried to include myself in this program, slipping the twelve steps away to read in private. The first step (admitted I was powerless over alcohol)—I stumbled right there, for why should I admit that? I was ready to admit my life was unmanageable. I was ready to do something about that. So I went hit and miss through them all.

"Sought through prayer and meditation" made me realize I

had been praying "my way," and then only when there seemed no other recourse. Soon, I realized that prayer, in order to become effective, must become as much a part of me as breathing. It is a living prayer when we do a task to our utmost. It is a prayer when we give hope and understanding to those in turmoil, as we were. It is a prayer when we think in the small watches of the night or in our quiet time. Prayer is living and loving life and my life must be governed by God, my family, my friends, and my associations. Responsibility for what happens to me or others lies in what I do or say and what I believe must stand the test of time to be productive.

I try by example to practice what I believe, as I believe every individual is under observation daily, as he or she moves among friends. Even the little things we do are scrutinized and our casual remarks weighed. Constantly do people take our measure. They may do more—they may fashion their conduct after our pattern to an extent they little admit. Our acts, of course, bring judgment upon ourselves, but with equal certainty they provide models more persuasive to others than studied argument.

No one, man or woman, of the humblest sort can really be strong, gentle, pure, and good without the world being the better for it, without someone being helped and comforted by the existence of this effort.

This would always swing me right back to the Fourth Step, "Make a searching and fearless moral inventory of ourselves." A prominent scientist has said there is enough atomic energy in our bodies to destroy the city of New York. "Know yourself," we are told. That means an analysis without fear and includes knowing our powers as well as our weaknesses. When we take an honest inventory, we get to know the tremendous power that is within us. We do not need to feel frustrated or defeated. So, again, we have "hope" instead of hopelessness on the right side of the ledger and have eliminated fear and frustration.

When we open our minds, a sense of power will come and we will wonder at the ease with which we meet responsibilities.

Capacity for work will increase, so will pleasure in accomplishment. Strain and tension will subside; again, we have "hope" balancing the scales.

With self-analysis we get to know what we expect of ourselves and what we are willing to give in return. So a good formula is to know what we want, test it to see if it is the right thing, then change ourselves in such a manner it will come naturally. This can be done if we expel negative thoughts and substitute positive thoughts in their place.

One of the first lessons I learned was we cannot hope to reconstruct without mistakes. I wanted everything, myself included, to become harmonious living. We may make many mistakes but will profit by them all, as we are at liberty to change our belief as often as we get new light. We can and should be willing to relinquish our former views and change our thoughts on any subject as often as wisdom furnishes us with enlightenment.

The philosophy of AA and Family Groups is not new. Most of us just lost it by the way. My first real jolt came when I could say a pleasant "goodbye" to my husband when he was going away. It was a revelation that I could say it and know it was not a bitter parting, but just a separation. Hopeless lost the "less" and I was so intrigued by that, I began in earnest my inventory.

Defects of character I would not admit, I was now forced to face. Family Groups or Al-Anon Groups as they are known in Montreal have only come in the last year. So coming to Toronto and attending the Scarborough Group with my husband, I was asked to come to a new Family Group forming there.

The first meeting I found others had resentments I thought exclusively mine; so one defect of character was easy to correct and thus lose. I have many yet and am working on them. Now I can "let go and let God." When we are willing to do what seems to us to be best and then leave the problem to Him, it will be solved. Many problems remain to be solved in our daily lives, but united in understanding and love we have a fullness of faith and hope never before known. We can now laugh together over former experiences. We find that the following of this program together moves us toward harmonious living.

In closing, I would like to use a portion of a letter written to me by my father, at a time when a teenage ego needed a guiding hand. I have found it so helpful in the past five years and thought it again might have a message. I quote:

It is very necessary now and then to put very pointed questions to oneself. Many find it most difficult to face up to these. We are so inclined to question others, not ourselves.

Self-examination is necessary because we can so easily slip back unconsciously, when all is well. Feelings can sometimes become frozen through pride and prejudice.

Spiritual stock-taking is urgent because our conception of sin may be imperfect. Most of us condemn the sin in others from which they deem themselves exempt. Some have more, some less of these to sweep away, but those who have the least still have something to do.

Therefore:
Count your blessings
Multiply your advantages
Add your endeavors and
Subtract your shortcomings.

And:
Sow a thought and you reap an act
Sow an act and you reap a habit
Sow a habit and you reap a character
Sow a character and you reap a destiny.

And always remember—each day brings:
Some duty that no one else can do
Some opportunity that will never come again
Some blows that cannot be avoided
Some defeats that seem final, but never are

Some reason for making a new fight for the right
Some encouragement to go in search of the best, and
Some responsibility that cannot be avoided.

These things AA associations and Family Groups have brought back into my life.

Thank you.[1]

COURAGE

Helen M.

The topic I have been given to discuss is "courage." Perhaps all of us do not give the word the same meaning. But the definition given in the dictionary is quite clear. "Courage" is defined as, "That quality of mind which shows itself in facing danger without fear." I will endeavor to tell you my interpretation of a new and workable meaning of "courage" that I have learned through my attendance at Family Group meetings.

When AA came into our lives some six years ago, I was just as frustrated, bewildered, and discouraged as most wives become who have lived this nightmare that goes to make up the upside-down existence of the alcoholic and his family. I was very happy in AA and thought it the most wonderful thing in the world. Just having friends again meant a great deal to me—we had had so few in recent years. At this stage I coasted along for a few months grateful for this newfound sobriety in our home.

It wasn't until I attended a panel put on by the wives, here in Toronto, that I realized this program could and would work for me also, with a little willingness and effort on my part. I will never forget that meeting and can still experience the enthusiasm I felt that night.

I had been attending meetings along with my husband,

but had never thought of putting the philosophy of Alcoholics Anonymous to work in my own life. I realized even then that I was no more equipped to face life than the alcoholic. Instead of escaping through alcohol, I would escape through any number of equally destructive and confused devices. The result is always the same—unhappy, discordant, unmanageable lives.

I started to attend the Family Group meetings in Hamilton and try to never miss our weekly meeting. It was then that AA moved right into our home and I believe I really started to learn to live. Little by little, as I withdrew from my shell and learned the true meaning of honesty and "keeping an open mind," the steps of Alcoholics Anonymous began to mean something to me personally. I was AMAZED to find that I had not been alone in my feeling of utter despair and discouragement left from the whiplash of alcoholism. I had thought that no one else in the world had ever experienced the awful fears and turmoil I knew so well.

Yet here was a group of girls who had a real understanding, gained only through their experience of my problems and reactions to them. They knew the distorted thinking brought about by living in a distorted atmosphere.

To be able to talk with others likewise twisted, and the chance to learn from them how their application of the AA program had helped them to regain self-respect and a normal attitude, was what I found in the Family Group. As I sought to apply the teachings of AA to my daily life, the first tool I tried to put into use was the Serenity Prayer. It, too, exemplifies what I understand as "courage"—the facing and acceptance of reality. This reality can include danger and a great deal of problems. You will remember that the prayer covers that same ground: "God, grant me the serenity to accept the things I cannot change; courage to change the things I can; and the wisdom to know the difference."

This prayer, to me, is the basis of a "way of life" as I try to live it today, and I say it many times during the day. In trying to accept things I cannot change, I have had to do a complete about-face.

Certainly I had not approached problems in any such spirit in the past. I had fought over them, suffered over them, never accepted them or my relationship to them. In my association with the group, I came to see I could "accept" happily. I came to the realization that I could not change anyone except myself. And wasn't it true that most of my unhappiness came from trying to change others to my way of thinking?

However, by my change of attitude and reactions to the happenings and problems of daily life, I can influence the atmosphere of our home. I had to accept the fact that much of the chaos and insecurity in our home resulted from my bad temper and behavior. It is out of this period that I feel I owe amends to my children. For the security that was rightfully theirs, regardless of our circumstances, the security they were denied. Still, I have learned that we can worry so much about the past that we are unable to enjoy what we have today. Yet we can do nothing about the past and so much about today, by constructive efforts.

Those who love us do not ask for restitution or reparation, but I feel that a sincere change of conduct, together with the newfound standard of values gained in AA, will surely help repay for all the impatience and intolerance I have had with those near and dear to me.

"Courage to change the things I can" has become a tremendous challenge to me. Attempting to live each twenty-four hours to the very fullest gives each day a feeling of great adventure and so has turned my life, which was once such a purposeless thing, into something worth living. And gee, it's good to be alive.

I, like most non-alcoholics, have always found it convenient to blame the alcoholic for my troubles. But each one of us, if fortunate enough to learn through AA or the Family Group, is finally forced to accept the fact that the main source of his troubles, and the only one he can control, lies within himself.

It took courage for me to take an honest appraisal of myself and admit that I had faults in my character makeup. Most of these defects I have had all my life and although no one except myself is aware of them they can surely be a block in my search for the full, rich life I know is possible by applying this program to the best of my ability.

My lack of self-confidence and inability to make even the smallest decision was certainly not conducive to a happy, positive way of living. It was much easier to admit these newfound personality weaknesses and failures than to do something about them. But being aware of them and not taking action is not trying—to the best of my ability—to find the answer to my problems.

In falling short and getting up and trying again, I have found that one of the main things "courage" requires of me is simply to "Keep on keeping on." If we have the wisdom to know what to accept and what to change and are willing to make an honest effort to do so, our lives will be happy and serene; I know.

But how can I be sure I have the wisdom to know the difference? Since coming into AA, troubles have certainly not passed us by. But by becoming aware of the guidance of my Higher Power—always doing the footwork, but always accepting the results as God's work—surely then, by asking for courage and strength to live each day as it comes, I will be given that thought or idea, that power to make a decision. On looking back, I only know that somehow, someway that Power came when I had to face the biggest disappointment in my life, and I was given the help to accept something that without AA would have filled me with hatred and resentment.

Well, I have talked a lot about courage. What you can do with it; what it can do for you. But where do you find it? I have found one special source of courage for me in the Family Groups. I made AA something I shared with my husband. Something we have become able to live and grow in together. There is no happier kind of oneness than that. It is a source and a great reward of courage.[2]

GROWTH

Babette B.

It is a great pleasure and a privilege to be speaking here this afternoon. Through the help and example of members of the Family Groups, my whole life has been changed in a most wonderful way. So it can't help but be a pleasure to be telling you about it.

My subject is "growth," and I know that this way of life is teaching us to "grow up." Some wives, I have no doubt, as they attend meetings with their husbands, realize they can apply the AA philosophy to themselves—not I. It was not until I went to the Family Groups that I learned to take the searchlight off my neighbor and turn it on myself.

For a long time I had been trying to reform my small world—a fruitless and frustrating business if ever I knew one. The knowledge that I could tackle my own defects and do something concrete was an invigorating challenge. As little by little my eyes were opened to my own shortcomings, I strived to do something about them. I gained a new kind of happiness I had never before known. As a result, I found I could be more lenient of other people's frailties. After all, I was discovering I had many.

It was wonderful to find that I was starting to grow up, that I need no longer be a slave to my emotions and that at my disposal were all kinds of help for spiritual growth. They say, "If we meet our problems, we are maturing; if we get emotional about them, we are failing." In trying to put this into practice, I am able to see situations in their true perspective, no longer as insurmountable hurdles. Somehow, as I keep calm, the problem diminishes in size. This is a normal, healthy way to live.

The slogan "First things first" has given me a new set of values. Through it I started to tidy up my life, to save myself from two enemies: "hurry" and "indecision." As I overcame small problems (such as whether I should make the bed or do the dishes first), I had more time and a clearer mind to see which things were really important and those to which I was giving undue importance. It wasn't pleasant to discover that through a wrong sense of values, I was being unloving. In AA I have discovered a new quality of love—a love which can let me forget myself and my feelings, which is at least trying to be patient. When we came to AA, I felt I was a model of patience. I have waited in a state of agitation, grinding my teeth and thinking, "How can anyone be so patient?"

Always wanting things left me so tired; I could not enjoy the things I had. Soon I realized that these were the things that were robbing me of peace of mind. As I no longer mentally stamp my feet to get my own way, things seem to work out so much better.

They say, "Dividends come on gratitude, not on defeat." I certainly can vouch for that. It was a turning point for me. I don't know of a more rewarding habit to cultivate than remembering to say "thank you." There is never a time so dark that I can't think of many things to be grateful for. When I count my blessings, they seem to multiply.

It was a great day for me when I found I need no longer be a victim of circumstances. Now I know that I can "set the mood." I need no longer let people or situations get me down. When they do, I'm the one who's going to pay for it. The times that I maintain my good humor, I'm helping myself; and, by so doing, I am available to be of service to others.

A willingness to develop a better understanding is coming into my life; and I hope that this continual process of growing will always be a part of my life. There is no standing still. If I'm not improving, I'll be slipping backwards. This is a program of progress, not perfection.

While I know my husband does not think I'm perfect, thank

goodness that he takes the trouble, once in a while, to point out some of my shortcomings. I now find it very helpful and a source for new resolve. What a difference from those days when the least disagreement had me up in arms! We both feel the other has improved considerably and our understanding has grown, as each in our own way, we have tried to put the AA principles to practice. It is so wonderful to have sobriety and all this too.

I would like, now, to say a few words especially for those of you whose alcoholic problem is still in the process of being solved. It was when there was a return to drinking in our home that I realized all that this program had done for me. I, who had always been so much a part of the disease, had gained new understanding and, with constant help, I was able to detach myself and leave my husband's problem.

One of the great sources of my trouble had been pride—pride expressed in covering up—in assuming someone else's responsibilities. So while I tried to cope with them in an ineffectual and misguided way, my own duties were left undone. This meant complete chaos reigned in our home. Instead of there being one person gone to pieces, there were two. Nor did I have the excuse of a disease—I was sober—but I certainly wasn't sane.

The things I had to do, which so changed the atmosphere, were all little things. When seen in the light of the twenty-four-hour program, they were even smaller. By "accepting the things I could not change," I was ridding myself of constant frustration. I don't know if all wives are the same, but I had spent so much time just laying myself wide open to frustration. So I learned that as I cooked dinner, I need not constantly be worrying about whether it was going to be eaten or not. That was not my end of the deal. Instead of doing everything against the grain, it was important for me to take real interest in my daily chores. I knew my attitude had to be right, or my peace of mind would leave me and fear would creep in. To keep my thinking clear, I now had two great courses I could consult: my Higher Power and my fellow members. Through reading, thinking, and trying to practice a positive way of life, what might have seen me re-adopt my old ways, turned into a period of real spiritual growth. There may be some wives here today with an active problem and I know there is help and hope for them here. Thank you.[3]

FAITH

Enid T.

I wish to express my thanks to those who asked me to take part in this panel discussion of the Family Group this afternoon. I feel it is a privilege and an honor. But I do feel a great sense of inadequacy to speak on the subject that was given to me: "faith."

In Harry Emerson Fosdick's book *On Being a Real Person,* in the chapter "The Practical Use of Faith," he says, "One way or another, in every realm, man is inherently a believer in something or other, positive or negative, good, bad, or indifferent." I agree with that. There is no vacuum in one's belief. Doubt, fear, resentment, and bitterness make up the negative. Humility, hope, courage, and action combine to make up the positive; and what we call faith is that positive which St. Paul expressed as "the substance of things hoped for, the evidence of things not seen." But I can only speak to you out of my own experience, giving you my own ideas, in the hope that they will make sense to someone here and be helpful.

When I first approached this program, I was not at all sure that it would have the answer for me or be of any help. I was separated from my husband because of alcohol, and so much seemed to have been destroyed that after two years I was physically and mentally ill. Because of my condition, my husband and I met to discuss our business arrangements. By this time he had found a solution to his drinking problem in AA and suggested that since he felt my condition had its roots in that alcoholic past perhaps the AA program could help me. If so, then we might consider trying to lead a normal life together. Well, I had nothing to lose by trying, and so I started.

Naturally, the first thing I was given to read and try to understand was the twelve steps of the AA program. The first step was self-evident. The second was something else again: "Came to believe that a Power greater than myself could restore me to sanity." I did believe that God (as I understood Him) could do this, but I doubted that He would. I was full of bitterness and unhappiness over things which had happened in the past, and when I tried to follow the suggestion of the fourth step and took a moral inventory of myself, I couldn't help feeling "why should He?"

I talked over these very real doubts and fears of mine with another member of the Family Group and she said to me, "What you need is faith." Yes, I could agree. But how does one begin to establish one's faith, to learn how to practice and use faith in everyday living?

She asked me to read a portion of Scripture, which I did, but somehow I found nothing to help me there. However, I was determined not to give up yet, and that night I continued to read at random and I came across a verse which meant a great deal to me then, and still does today.

"But if any man draw back, my soul shall find no pleasure in him." The phrase "any man" was in italics so even I felt I could fit myself in. Somehow this gave me a positive direction in how to live the twenty-four-hour program. I had been told that I must not dwell on yesterday, I must not think of tomorrow, I must live today. But yesterday and tomorrow had taken a great deal of my time and energy in today and this phrase gave me some idea of how to positively fill the void if yesterday and tomorrow were to be deleted from my day. In other words, I must try to do or to think or to act in some way so that at the end of the day I could feel that God, as I understood Him, might find some pleasure in it.

Perhaps it was only making the effort to plan and carry through with a treat for the children, or even making a special dessert. I was in no position, physically or mentally, to make any sweeping gestures and I learned that so often that is precisely what most of us are looking for. We wait for some large opportunity, sometimes defined, sometimes undefined, and in the waiting so many little, small, seemingly insignificant things slip by. Now I realize as well as you do that making a chocolate cake or a peach pie did not solve my whole problem, but I found that my small gestures were not despised, for I was given the strength and the guidance to carry out larger things when they came with more poise than I had had for many a long day.

Getting out of the past grew easier day by day with this definite focus, and I could see that any thought and all talk of it was no good and had to be left behind, where it belonged. And then, little by little, this same guiding point dissolved apprehension of the future. "Sufficient unto the day is the evil thereof." And you know, because of my motto, it wasn't too long before I could smile, even at myself. For really, one doesn't meet very many soul-shaking problems in a week. That tendency to make mountains out of molehills, to build things up with supposing, which happens to all who have been gripped by fear, began to disappear. For you simply can't smile at yourself and be afraid at the same time.

Make no mistake, I did not sprout wings and I have no halo. I am just an ordinary human being with many shortcomings and character defects, some of them very well developed, and I made a lot of mistakes. I did not always adhere 100% to this idea of twenty-four-hour living, but while it is true one never graduates from this program, one is never expelled either.

The tenth step seems to take care of our natural human frailties: "Continued to take personal inventory and when we are wrong, promptly admit it." I found it to be true from my own experience what I had heard Tom say some six years ago, "You cannot out-do the Lord in loving kindness." Opportunities are always at hand and if you feel you've flubbed one, say you're sorry or make your amend and keep going, try again.

I hesitate to say that one step in this program is more important than another and yet, to me, the eleventh step is the pillar. I found it to be a tremendous exercise of mind: "Sought through prayer and meditation to improve my conscious contact with God as I understood Him." To the best of my ability, I have tried to follow that suggestion and if you are like me, with a well-developed sense of what you think other people should do, you will find it a tremendous exercise in self-discipline—"praying only for knowledge of His will for me and the power to carry that out." To practice, and mind my *own* business and leave others to do the same. In other words, I began to see the point of "Live and let live" and that gave me a great sense of freedom and peace of mind.

Have I talked to you about faith? I don't really know, but I have tried to give you some idea of how I started, with the help of this program, to live by faith. Knowing as I do that my husband practices and uses this program in his way of life, and acknowledging, as he does, my attempt to use it to the best of my ability in my daily life, we have a basis of cooperation, a feeling of companionship, of mutual respect which has blossomed into a very normal and happy life. I am very grateful that I can say I "came to believe that a Power greater than myself could restore me to sanity."[4]

FIVE

Laying the Foundation for Al-Anon

Before a centralized clearinghouse or service center was established, each Family Group was completely on its own. The groups were responsible for everything—establishing a name, program, literature, meeting format, location, and public awareness. Most groups used the AA Twelve Steps with minimal revisions. Some of the more established groups sent mimeographed literature to newer groups to help them get started, since as one long-time member told me, "We just didn't have any money and we relied heavily on the AA group for support."[1]

I could locate nothing to indicate exactly where the following two handwritten documents originated; however, I have reason to believe they came from one of the very early California groups, possibly in Long Beach. I've made only nominal changes to correct spelling, grammar, and so on, providing clarity while leaving the content unchanged. Simply titled "AA Auxiliary Ritual," the first of these documents is a meeting format.

AA AUXILIARY RITUAL

"Tonight, I am acting as chairman of this auxiliary meeting of Alcoholics Anonymous, as is customary in the alcoholic group. I will first introduce myself: my name is _____ and I am here in the interest of my husband/son/brother/father/wife/daughter/sister or mother, who is an alcoholic.

"We are gathered here as relatives of alcoholics to learn all we can about alcoholism; how we may be able to help our alcoholic loved one through the convalescent period of that illness; and to share our understanding of at least one problem common to each of us—namely, to share the experience of a complex disease in our families (a sickness of the mind, body, and emotions) which devastates not only the alcoholic but to some extent the entire household. It is estimated that with the recovery of one alcoholic, twenty people get well. We have tried many ways to lick this problem; we have poured out liquor, watered it, hidden it; we have nagged, pled with, threatened, and sometimes left the alcoholic. We have fumed, and we have prayed, all to no avail, unless our prayers have been answered by this AA program.

"For the privilege of this meeting and for this new hope of recovery, we owe gratitude to the program of AA. It is our duty to read and study the "Big Book" *[Alcoholics Anonymous]* and all other AA literature we can secure, in order that we may be families with the AA "Way of Life" and understand how it can help both our sick ones and ourselves toward a happier, serene life.

"This auxiliary, like the Alcoholic Group, is open to all faiths. While the AA program contains six spiritual steps, no doctrine or faith is discussed: only silent prayer or meditation and "The Lord's Prayer" are ever used in meetings. Our alcoholic turns his life over to a Higher Power as he understands it. Likewise, each of us here pays tribute and thanks to a Higher Power as we individually understand it. Non-believers, Jewish, Catholic, and Protestant followers are members of AA—therefore all are welcome to this auxiliary.

"Of prime importance in AA Tradition, as stressed by one of the co-founders of AA, is the anonymous feature of the program. Not only should the new member realize her obligation to respect and keep the anonymity of the alcoholic, of the auxiliary, and of any and all of their activities, but she is entitled to know that we also will respect and maintain the anonymity of her interest in AA. There are good reasons for this attitude: the new alcoholic member in the group often feels himself to be a social failure or outcast; naturally, he does not wish to be thus publically identified. Another and deeper reason is that the principles of the AA program mean more than the personalities trying to follow it. Within the group we identify and understand the alcoholics; outside of it they are anonymous. AA policy says, "A member may admit his own fellowship with AA but under no circumstances should he reveal the name of any other member." Our auxiliary should be guided by that policy.

"Two other points are especially important; the new alcoholic member desperately needs sweets (candies, cakes, desserts) to help replace the sugar content of alcohol he is now leaving off. Also, we need to banish all feelings of embarrassment and stigma. Public ignorance stamps the alcoholic as a weakling or moral failure, but for our peace of mind and because it is true, we must help our alcoholic understand that he has an "illness" to overcome and not a moral degeneration.

"As an auxiliary group we should present to the alcoholics themselves for approval any ideas or projects we have for social activities, and abide by their decisions. Before proceeding with the discussion of the evening, we shall now have a minute of silent prayer or meditation."

After this minute of reflection, there is a discussion lesson on an AA talk or whatever the program is for the evening—always on AA.

Business: reports, etc.

Announcements: birthdays, parties, next meeting place, etc.

Close meeting with The Lord's Prayer.[2]

AS YOU CAN SEE from this format, the wives' groups were very much a part of AA in those early days. I'm certain that this particular meeting format was not used in all locations. It's very likely that each group selected a format with which members were comfortable. It's easy to see why Bill W. strongly encouraged Lois to pull the groups together to develop their own unified fellowship.

The following handwritten document is from the same anonymous person. It seems fitting to provide you with this example, which clearly demonstrates that the non-alcoholics had a program of their own.

This version of the Twelve Steps differs considerably from the original version used by AA and the version now used by Al-Anon Family Groups. I believe these Steps reflect the thoughts of one group—likely written by one founding member of the group.

NAA TWELVE STEPS
NON-ALCOHOLICS ANONYMOUS

First—I admitted that I was powerless over an alcoholic and that our lives had become unmanageable. (Hadn't I spent ____ years trying to change our alcoholic without success? Hadn't I used pleas, reproaches, love, hate, threats, and reasoning, wept, laid awake nights worrying and praying? Certainly both of our lives had become unmanageable in the chaotic state in which we were living.)

Second—Came to believe that a Power greater than ourselves could restore me to sanity. (If I was to be restored to sanity, it must be through a Power greater than myself, for certainly I was on the verge of insanity after living for ___ years with an alcoholic. What else could a life that is made up of fears, suspicion, antagonism, dishonesty, and distrust be, if not insanity?)

Third—Made a decision to turn my life over to God whether I understand Him or not. (Why should I attempt to understand God? I know that much of my confusion over religion has been due to the belief that I should accept a given interpretation of Him—that I was unable to accept these interpretations and that now I would turn my life over to this power or force or God whether I understand it or not.)

Fourth—Made a searching and fearless moral inventory of myself. (In this I made some shocking discoveries—I found that over a period of years, while living with an alcoholic, and the accompanying worry, strain, distress, and unhappiness which is the natural result of such a life, I had built up a pattern of living that was no credit to me or my character.)

Fifth—Admit to God, myself, and other human beings the nature of my mistakes.

(I had become apprehensive of the future.

1. I threw up a cloud of fear and worry that engulfed me every time I was away from my husband or he was away from me.
2. I mistrusted him and showed the mistrust.
3. I had become irritable and nervous.
4. I had grown less affectionate [through repulsion].
5. I condemned rather than praised.
6. Above all, I had developed self-pity and hurt pride that was driving me away from society, friends, and God.)

Sixth & Seventh—I am entirely ready for God to remove all

these defects of character, and humbly ask Him to remove my shortcomings.

Eighth—I am willing to make amends for the mistakes of the past, to constantly be on the alert for any destructive habits, such as nagging and criticizing.

Ninth—When wrong I will promptly admit it. (This is hard to do for usually we think we are right. I was wrong to show my understanding of an alcoholic—in fact, wrong in my whole attitude of living.)

Tenth—I will continue to take personal inventory. (This I must do to keep me from developing these defects of character which through habit may creep back into my life. I must re-educate myself, I must grow with my husband, and I must constantly be honest with myself.)

Eleventh—I will seek through prayer and meditation to improve my conscious contact with God. (I am conscious of the Power many times during the day and through this contact I am eliminating pettiness, distrust, fear, antagonism, and self-pity from my life.)

Twelfth—Having had this spiritual experience through the help and fellowship of AA and having had my heart warmed and my soul fed by friendliness and love as exhibited in this organization, it is my earnest desire to carry this message to others and to practice these principles in all my affairs.[3]

THE EARLY FAMILY GROUPS attempted to separate themselves from AA and for the most part were quite successful in doing so. This new, independent endeavor created certain challenges as to how to operate an effective organization using the AA principles without interfering with the Alcoholics Anonymous group. The Family Groups were thus forced to create their own inexpensive literature that would help them spread the word.

Many groups started with brief handouts, usually two pages, which were printed either on card stock or plain paper, creased, and folded. For titles, these pieces generally used the name of the particular group publishing the piece. Several examples are shown here. The first is a "card" from Vancouver.

Front cover: **NAA**
Inside: **GUIDE TO NON-ALCOHOLICS ANONYMOUS OF GREATER VANCOUVER**

OBJECTS
1. To promote fellowship, unite and advance the interests of the wives of AA members: to foster their progress back to a happy life.
2. To help the AA wives understand their husbands and their problems.

CODE OF ETHICS
Anyone entering this Association hereby incurs the obligation of upholding its dignity and honour and preserving its high standards by refusing to repeat outside the meetings any part of that which has been discussed.[4]

THE TORONTO FAMILY GROUPS developed a very informative thirty-page pamphlet that was then circulated to many other groups. The pamphlet reveals that the Toronto groups had developed into a very solid organization. Here are some highlights from the pamphlet's brief chapters.

FAMILY GROUPS OF AA

God grant me the serenity
To accept the things I cannot change
Courage to change things I can,
And the wisdom to know the difference.

WHY A FAMILY GROUP?

These questions are often asked:

1. What is a Family Group?
2. What is its purpose?
3. Who needs this group?

The Family Groups, or Wives' Groups, as they were originally called, are groups of women made up mostly of wives, members, or friends of an alcoholic's family. These people have a sincere desire to understand the AA program, and to change their own character pattern with the help of the twelve steps of AA.

Many of us have come to realize that such groups are a spiritual force. Through personal application we have found the following results:

A return of confidence—confidence in the power of God, in people, and in one's self.

Strength to keep on keeping on.

Courage to face one's self, life, and the problems which confront us.

Patience, with the realization that "All things work together for good to those who love God."

GOD IS LOVE

Love is very patient,
Love is very kind,
Love knows no jealousy,
Love makes no parade,
Love gives itself no airs,
Love is never rude,
Love is never selfish,
Love is never irritated,
Love is never resentful,
Love is never glad when others go wrong,
Love is always gladdened by goodness,
Love is slow to expose,
Love is eager to believe the best,

Love is always hopeful,
Love is always patient,
Love never faileth.

Now put your own name in place of the word LOVE and read the love chapter again.

SUGGESTED PLAN FOR FAMILY GROUP MEETINGS

Our meetings are conducted according to the pattern of the regular AA meetings.

1. We start with a moment's silence, followed by the AA prayer.
2. The chairman states the purpose of the meeting and welcomes the newcomers.
3. The chairman presents the topic of the meeting and gives her understanding of it. She then invites the members to take part in the discussion, keeping the meeting on the subject at hand.
4. We close the meeting with the Lord's Prayer.

Our meetings last approximately an hour, followed by tea and cookies. Over a friendly cup of tea there is the opportunity for more personal contact, during which time experiences may be shared, if anyone desires to do so.

As there is no organization in Family Groups, the responsibility of chairman is shared by various members.

We have found the success of Family Groups depends on:

- Not discussing our husbands,
- Respecting any confidences,
- Preserving anonymity.[5]

ONE OF THE FIRST PUBLISHED NEWSLETTERS for the Family Groups originated in San Francisco, with Ruth G. as the editor. It was entitled *The Family Forum*. This name was later slightly changed to *Family Group Forum* and adopted by the Clearing House for its newsletter in September 1954.

The San Francisco Family Forum was published monthly and contained twelve pages of discussion of family problems arising from alcoholism. The following is an example of a typical discussion; this one was found in the November 1952 issue.

Question: My husband, who is still drinking, says he is ill and that I should be very considerate of him. Do I have to treat him like a baby as he demands?

Discussion: A poll would no doubt show that as an excuse for drinking, "illness" rates highest. What wife hasn't had it used at one time or another? These "ill" ones are indeed truly ill, morally and spiritually, even unto death, but they skip all that. They miss the whole significance of their illness.

They don't go into any uncomfortable analysis of their illness or make any attempt to be healed by the power of God: they seize upon the words "I am ill" to put themselves into a special category which demands of the world, "Look at me! *I* am ill—so now *you'd* better be nice to me, and not cross me, or deny me anything, or expect anything of me."

So they sew themselves up in a big bag of insularity and try to reign as piddling little despots in their small world, while their dreadful cancerous illness eats away at their souls.

You don't know what to do? You can't do anything, of yourself. Turn your own life and your own will over to the care of God, and remember that under the burden of this surface "illness" of your husband's is a real illness in which you have a part, under God's direction, to fulfill. This is a training ground and proving ground for *you*. You would not have been given this particular relationship if you were not yourself spiritually ill.

Your concern is with yourself, and the healing of your own illness. In the meantime, how to live with the "illness," as he is seeing it, of your husband? As your own illness is healed, the way will be made clear to you. The problem cannot be solved by any human means. The solution must transcend anything we know. It lies in the hands of God.

You don't have to treat him like a baby, as he demands. You may have to stand by and help him while he learns not to act like a baby; that is a different thing than babying him. (He probably won't like it!)[6]

ALSO FOUND IN THE SAME NEWSLETTER was a quote from Lois W. of Bedford Hills, New York: "The more visiting from group to group we can all do, the closer we will all feel. At the same time with knowledge and understanding of each other the panorama widens of the tremendous scope of this great movement of ours."[7]

The following is the opening paragraphs from the September 1954 *Family Group Forum.*

Dear Friends,

Have you noticed our new name? It was the favorite in our recent poll of groups for an appropriate name for our newsletter.

Forums in ancient days were places where people met to do business, hold law courts, and decide public matters. Our *Family Group Forum* can be a real meeting place of all groups, via the written word, and will be truly representative only when all of you contribute to it.[8]

AL-ANON FAMILY GROUPS has continued to publish a newsletter every month since Lois W. and Anne B. first began corresponding with the groups under the name "Clearing House."

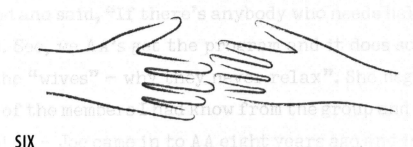

SIX

"I Knew It Was Time to Tell My Story": Margaret D.

Margaret D. was the first editor of the Al-Anon monthly news-letter *Family Group Forum*, today a magazine known as *The Forum*. She was a dedicated member of Al-Anon throughout her life and worked tirelessly in the early days alongside Lois W. (her sponsor), Anne B., and the other volunteers at Clearing House, which was then housed in the old AA 24th Street Clubhouse. Margaret was the sponsor of my dear friend, Arbutus O. Both of these ladies enjoyed traveling, being involved in service through the Al-Anon fellowship, and working with others. Each of them was invited to speak at conferences throughout the world. In my archives are a hundred-plus letters between the two of them that give witness to their friendship and their dedicated lives.

Through the years, I've heard many people say that they are just the instrument being used by God to do His work. As I researched Margaret D., I could feel a tremendous power working through her life as she carried a message of hope to potentially thousands of Family Group members through her dedicated service.

Margaret shared her story at the fifth Al-Anon rally held in Detroit, Michigan. The following is adapted from that talk.

•••••••••••••

If anybody ever had a drastic change in her character, I am that person. Before I share anything I would like to make it clear that anything I say is absolutely my own opinion and interpretation; this is what has helped me. Therefore, I won't be talking about my husband, though he does enjoy traveling with me. If I do say something it's not breaking his anonymity, only sharing my own experience.

I also would like to make it clear that it was my failure to solve a difficult personal situation which made the very great change in my personality and in my character. If I had had Al-Anon from the time I was first married, I think perhaps I would have been a different person. I don't know this for sure and it's really not important because I did find Al-Anon when I most bitterly needed it. I thank God that I did find it.

My own personal difficulties began before I was married. My mother was very much a "live and let live" type of person. But one day she said to me, "Margaret, aren't you a little worried about Jack's drinking?"

My response was, "Oh Mother, that's nonsense. It's just that he's alone so much—the minute we're married he'll stop drinking." I really believed this and felt that just being married to me would be enough to change him.

Now I don't say he's an alcoholic. He says he is and also believes that his alcoholism started when he was a teenager. I did, however, notice very shortly after we were married that his drinking was different from mine. I had always had a lot to drink and enjoyed it. Growing up there was alcohol in our home.

But I found that my husband's drinking was entirely different.

I could take it or leave it alone and he couldn't do either one. If we had a few drinks before dinner—we had a lot of drinks after dinner. I would stop because I just couldn't stand the effects, but he could not stop until the bottle was empty and sometimes not even then.

Gradually his drinking progressed and seemed to overshadow everything else. I was very upset. We were living in Paris at the time which is where my daughter was born. Around this time the opportunity came for us to go out to the western Rockies to operate a horse and cattle guest ranch. This was exciting for me because I had spent four summers out on this ranch before we were married. Of course I'm thinking, "Boy, this is the answer we need. If he's in Montana, eighty miles from the nearest liquor store, he'll stop."

So rather than directly talk with him, being honest about my desire to relocate for a geographic cure to his drinking, I explained to him that it absolutely killed me that I would say something in English to our daughter and she would answer me in French. I told him I thought she should be brought up in her own country. Now Jack had spent a lot of time in the army and this outdoor life intrigued him and he was as excited about the move as I was.

Of course, he had no idea that I was trying to reform his character. So off we went to Montana! I think I had one week of physics during my life and I believe that was the week when they covered that water seeks its own level; and believe me you can't keep alcohol away from alcoholics. They can get to their own level quicker than water can. Here I was, eighty miles from town and five miles from the nearest railroad—surrounded by plenty of liquor. My grand scale change hadn't had any effect.

Then the army came calling and if you have ever worried that your husband would say the wrong thing to the commander and you would end up renting an apartment near Fort Leavenworth waiting for him to be released [from jail for insubordination], you know how I felt! Well, that didn't happen and he did all right, although his drinking continued and was heavy.

After the war ended he went back to his old agency, this time in the New York office. I was raised in the Midwest in a large family. I had always been afraid of Easterners, thinking they were very conventional, cold, and critical. As it turned out, I loved them—we had wonderful neighbors. But by this time his drinking had progressed and I was really a mess. I could no longer answer the door or the telephone; I was scared to meet people and I was bitterly unhappy.

This went on until one Sunday morning, when I was walking to church, I got about halfway there and suddenly got to "the end." I looked up and said, "God, you will have to help me. I cannot do it alone." I remember saying this out loud. I should also tell you just how screwy my thinking was at the time. The Yonkers bar that my husband drank at didn't open on Sundays until 1:00 p.m. I was hurrying to attend the 7:00 a.m. mass so I could get home and try to keep him from leaving for the bar. I was just hysterical!

I continued on my way to church and by some fortunate coincidence it happened to be Pentecost Sunday and the Epistle was about the Holy Spirit coming down and strengthening the apostles and giving them light. And I thought, "All of my life I've prayed to the Father and to the Son, but I've completely ignored the Holy Ghost. If anybody ever needed strengthening and enlightening, I was that person.

Well, I began praying and I believe it was only a few feet from where I had stopped and yelled at God that He spoke to me. I heard the words "AA!" This happened in 1947. I remembered that six years earlier I had read an article in the *Saturday Evening Post* by Jack Alexander about Alcoholics Anonymous and these people who had some magic cure to alcoholism through Twelve Steps. Of course, my thinking at the time was that these were do-gooders and it probably didn't work anyway.

Sometime later, my husband, while still in the service, attended a business meeting in Denver and was probably drinking quite heavily. Upon his return I was preparing his clothes for the laundry and a piece of paper with the words "Alcoholics Anonymous" and a Denver phone number fell out. I thought, "Oh, this is that thing I read about. If I ever get to where they are, I'm going to find them and talk to them." (This was while we were still in Montana.)

Here I was years later, living in Yonkers and AA finally came into my mind. I went home and I don't know if anyone else has ever felt the way Jack did that morning—just waking up with the king of all hangovers. All he wanted was peace and quiet and I came walking into the bedroom excitedly explaining to him that he has a problem. His drinking is not normal and there are people who can help. I suggested he call AA. Well, he would have nothing to do with it. I continued for probably an hour, until in frustration I shouted, "Either you go to AA or else!" Then I stormed out of the room.

A while later Jack called me in and said, "Okay, will you call them for me?" I did, and a short time later a couple of men showed up and they were simply stupendous. They talked, and the following night he went with them to a meeting. He continued to go to meetings and was very excited about them. He loved it; he began to tell me about the two men who called on him. For the first time I was beginning to appreciate and understand that alcoholism is a disease. I saw that it wasn't willfulness, or meanness to me. It wasn't deliberate; it was something as out of his control as something could be. This was the first time I saw hope for us!

After a short while he invited me to go to AA meetings with him. Of course I went and I loved them. AA never had a promoter like me—I would look Bill W. in the eye and tell him what a marvelous program this was. If AA's would just practice this way of life there wouldn't be any war, meanness, or crime. There would be nothing but sweetness and light. This was the Golden Rule and this is how we were meant to live.

Do you think that I ever practiced it myself? No, it was the AA program; it was labeled that and devised for alcoholics and I wasn't an alcoholic. I would have worked the program if anyone had suggested it, but nobody did. I would have tried to, but the idea had just never crossed my mind that a non-alcoholic could do any more than give lip service to it and so that is what I gave it.

For almost nine months things were wonderful, and then my husband changed jobs. It was the best job he had ever had and he became fearful that somebody might see him go into an AA meeting. Now, I know he hadn't given it quite long enough because we know this was really unhealthy thinking. But that was what he thought and he stopped going to meetings. He lasted two or three months before he started drinking again. In those two or three months, I had relaxed almost completely, life had been marvelous. I thought with such a program as this how could it fail or how could anybody fail it. I don't think AA has ever failed anyone. I think it is the people—I think I'm the one who failed it!

Things got worse than they had ever before been. I knew much more about what alcohol could do now. I always thought DTs were something you joked about and found in the comic section of the newspapers. I had never before heard of wet-brains, or even blackouts. So now armed with my knowledge, I was truly a real mess.

Fortunately, it wasn't too long until one of my AA friends, one of the women from the group, called me. She told me that there was something new—she wasn't sure exactly what it was all about—but it was for the families of alcoholics. This was in 1951. She continued and said, "If there's anybody who needs help it's those families. See, we AA's get the program and it does something to us, but the 'wives'—why they never relax." She began to point out some of the members I had known from the group and said, "Look at so-and-so. Joe came into AA eight years ago and is doing fine, but Joann, his wife, is as nervous as she was the night he came in."

She continued to go right around the group with comments on each of the wives. I thought, "Gee, I'm not so relaxed myself — maybe I'm the one who needs it."

She informed me that this new group needed help; they had far more work than two people could do and perhaps I would like to help by giving some time. I said that I would love to give some time.

She told me to call Lois. This was all I needed because one of our AA members had been doing a special project with Bill Wilson and would go to the Wilsons' house every week to work on it. One night while visiting our house, Dick happened to mention that he felt Bill was marvelous, but he said, "Sometimes I think that little Lois has more on the ball."

Well, I was just completely astounded. I thought if the person who had helped to think up this AA program wasn't the smartest person in the world, I wanted to see somebody who was a bit smarter. This was my chance!

After calling Lois the very next day, I went down to the old Clearing House. At that time there were only four of us who were regular volunteers. They had just moved the operation from the Wilson home in the country to the AA 24th Street Clubhouse. They had Irma, who would come in part-time in the afternoons to help Lois, and Anne, who had been doing the work at Stepping Stones up to this point. We also had Dottie, and then me. So the four of us were the four regulars and they asked me what I could do.

I said, "I can do anything in an office." So they had me opening the mail, reading it, and typing responses to the inquiries. They gave me a stack of sample paragraphs which I was to use for answers and said if I got into any trouble to ask them. I answered a lot of mail from people wanting to know about literature, or where other groups were, which were sparse, and of course people wanting advice. Keep in mind that I hadn't yet even attended a meeting.

Every day I would pack my lunch, show up, and start. I worked like a zombie. I wouldn't talk unless I had a question; I'd barely look up. I managed to get a lot of work accomplished simply reading the letters thoroughly and taking a prewritten paragraph from a stack prepared for me by Lois or Anne and using them to create the reply. If I ever ran into anything beyond me, I would ask for help.

The others in the office were concerned about me because I was so silent. I think they were afraid I was going to break. In time, through doing this work, Al-Anon began to enter even my thick brain. It was three months before I ever went to a meeting—if anyone has ever come in through the back door, it was me.

Throughout this entire time, always on my mind was this intolerable burden I was carrying and wouldn't share with anyone. I had been so bad and there wasn't anything I hadn't tried to do to make Jack stop drinking. There had been a parade of doctors through our house—I did these things in spite of AA. I did everything. I got people from the Yonkers AA group to go out at times to help me find him. And when things got so desperate and I was too ashamed to ask for help, I went out on my own to find him, leaving our daughter home alone. Occasionally I would find him, but even then, what was I to do?

I even had a hypnotist come with his wife, and use soft lights and music. I tried everything; except, of course, there was one thing I never did and that was *to do nothing*. I always had a project, believing that somehow this time it would work. I would tell myself, "I just haven't hit on the right thing yet."

Of course, all this behavior was while I was working at the office for those three months. We have miracles of coincidence in Al-Anon, just as they do in AA. One particular night, after working in the office, I attended my first Al-Anon meeting.

I should tell you that I had grown very superstitious and

quite neurotic in my thinking. Jack would go out of town to Philadelphia on Wednesday mornings for work. This was also the day that our laundryman would come to pick up the linens and I would change the beds. Well, when Jack completed his work, he always decided to have a few drinks. His justification was that he was out of town so nobody would know. This would start him going again, and again.

Now, here's how insane my thinking had become. I associated my changing the bed linens with his trips to Philadelphia. So I no longer would change the beds (even when he wasn't out of town) because I was afraid he would start drinking. Please understand, I knew this didn't make sense and it was wrong— but nothing on earth could make me change those beds. I was completely embarrassed by this and my other behaviors so that I just wouldn't talk to anyone about anything.

So there I was at my first meeting and a beautiful, little, blue-eyed Irish girl stood up to speak in front of about twenty people—which I couldn't imagine. She began to tell her story. Laughing, she said, "I'm the type of person who thinks if there is one smudge on my curtains the entire house needs to be cleaned. But I learned to live with my curtains a good battleship grey because every time I washed them my husband started a binge."

Everyone in the room laughed, but not me! I was frozen—I couldn't move. I just sat there confused and thinking, "How could this girl have done such a shameful thing and speak of it in public?" Yet somewhere inside of me I thought, "If she can do it, maybe I can too." She went on to say that her husband was what they called a periodic drinker and it was only coincidental that some of his binges began during times when she was cleaning the house.

Her story really struck me and I felt hopeful. The next morning I got up and changed the beds—this was my first victory! I still wasn't able to tell anyone about it. I drove into New York with Lois to go to the Clearing House and we would talk about everything—she was very easy to talk to. But I kept this a secret; I just couldn't tell her or anyone else about those sheets. I was ashamed.

When I had about six months in the program, the Montclair, New Jersey, Al-Anon group invited me to speak at their meeting. This would be my first time and I've always been grateful to them for giving me the opportunity. I was, of course, very nervous and I really didn't know what I would say when I got up there to speak. On the bus ride over, the memory of the little Irish girl telling about her curtains popped into my head and I remembered the courage she had to tell that story which helped me so much. I knew it was time to tell my story of the "sheets" and I did.

After the meeting a lady quickly came up to me, threw her arms around me, and thanked me. She said, "I'm so glad you were here tonight. I needed to hear what you said and I'm going home right now to roast a chicken."

"Oh," I said, "so it's the roast chicken, my sheets, and so-and-so's lace curtains." With a smile she said, "Yes," and told me her story. Several others approached me that night and shared similar stories of their experiences.

It wasn't until I had been in the program for over a year that I could honestly and completely take the First Step. I could see where my life was "unmanageable," but I just couldn't get the "powerless over alcohol" part. I thought I was just stupid or naïve—always thinking that if I just try this or try that I'll find the right way to get him to stop.

One day at the office I mentioned to my friend Dottie that I was dreading going home because I just knew he'd been drinking. She looked at me and said, "Why don't you work on the First Step? You're powerless, what can you do about it?"

I began to make progress with the program and things got better. Once in awhile I would think, "I've got it! Now, I really have it!" I would have a glimmer of it, but then when faced with difficult times I'd slip back into old ways and do something to try to control him and his drinking. I did manage to get to the point where I stopped throwing out bottles and stealing his money so he couldn't drink. I learned that nobody can keep an alcoholic from drinking when he really wants to drink.

Finally, after three years in Al-Anon and all the ups and downs at home, I was able to accept the First Step. I was headed to the subway for my ride home and knew that, again, he was drinking and had been for a few days.

I remembered a story one of the women had told about how she bought three bottles of liquor and placed them on the table in the bedroom so her husband would see them when he got up. Her husband woke up, saw the bottles there, and walked right over to the phone and called AA. He said, "I need help! My wife's trying to make me an alcoholic."

My mind was telling me to stop and pick up six bottles to take home because I was just so desperate. As I stood there waiting for a light to cross the street for the liquor store, the thought came to me, "Are you ever going to take the First Step? Are you ever going to take your hands off him and let him solve his own problem? That is what AA is for—Al-Anon is for you. Now let him do his and you take care of your own problem."

Things weren't always easy from then on out and I don't think they ever are. I've never read in any books that this life is for anything more than to teach us spiritual growth. I believe this is really what this program is for.

I certainly didn't do everything right, but what I learned I did share with my daughter—all that I could. She was in college when I came into Al-Anon and I remember telling her that this is a disease, once I understood that it was. When she had vacation from school, she would ask if she could visit the group and she was always most welcome. She became a regular member. She really lived the program and I think she took the First Step before she really even knew what it was. She seemed to have an instinctive comprehension of what the program really was. I know of experiences she had attending college where she applied the principles from this program and helped many of the girls who were suffering from various problems. It was a joy to see her graduate and be surrounded by so many friends.

My work at the Al-Anon office evolved and I became the editor of our newsletter, *The Forum*. This has allowed me the chance to give back a little of what has been freely given to me. I believe that is how it is with both AA and Al-Anon—we give it forward. I could never go back and repay those people who added to my sanity—like the little Irish girl with the curtains. I think I pay it back by helping the next one. We can always give somebody a "lift," which is my way of paying it forward.[1] ⌒

MARGARET REMAINED THE EDITOR of *The Forum* until her retirement in 1974. She traveled all over the world with her sober husband and enjoyed her many Al-Anon friends. In a typed speech she gave to Arbutus, Margaret reminisced about her life and those early days when Al-Anon was only a handful of volunteers and a rapidly growing fellowship of groups.

Here are some of her memories. This speech is excerpted here since much of the personal information has already been shared.

. . . .

Lois asked a friend, Anne, to help her and they started on a list of people and a few groups which had written to the AA General Service Office. That was March of 1951. We used to say June, but Lois says it was March. They worked in an upstairs room at Stepping Stones, the Wilson home in Bedford Hills. They began with little or nothing to work with—no letterhead, no literature, nothing but courage and determination to help anyone who lived with the problem of alcoholism.

It was a fertile field and by fall, they were looking for quarters in Manhattan. Work had increased so greatly that they couldn't keep up with it, and in Westchester County they couldn't get help. So on January 9, 1952, they moved to the old 24th Street

Clubhouse. There, a large upper room was available to them during the day, while AA used it at night. . . .

Upon my arrival the first day at the Clearing House, I reluctantly pushed the hard-to-find doorbell and Anne came down to let me in. We would be working alone that day, because Lois and Dot were attending the annual luncheon of the National Committee on Alcoholism. We walked together down that long hallway that the AA's called "the last mile" and up the steepest, narrowest stairs I've ever climbed. We entered a large room never meant for an office. The far end had been partitioned off into two rooms, both small. One had a regular roll-top desk and the oldest existing typewriter; the other had a dressing table and coat tree in it. Bill occasionally slept there when meetings of General Service lasted very late.

Lois and Bill had lived here in the early AA days before their move to Stepping Stones, but nothing remained of their stay. Lois told us about the dresser drawers she had made from orange crates, of the curtains she hung to make closets, and other improvisations. Stepping Stones must have been heaven after that.

Larry M., an artist and an AA member, was sort of in charge of the Clubhouse and, like all of us, ardently admired Bill. One morning Lois was horrified when we came in and found a crimson velvet rope, like those in museums, stretched across the open door so that one could see into "Bill's room" but not profane it by entering. Lois said, "This looks like a shrine. I'll have to do something about it before Bill sees it. He'll have a fit." Lois knew of Larry's admiration of Bill, but also knew that any fuss made over him would embarrass him. How she succeeded in getting rid of the velvet rope without hurting Larry's feelings, I'll never know, but I'd guess it's what makes Lois, Lois. AA's from all over the world always came to the Clubhouse when in New York, and always visited Bill's room.

Larry, like Bill, was one of Al-Anon's earliest and most ardent admirers. For some time a great many AA's were violently against our movement. That was annoying but very understandable; few wives, pre-family groups had been understanding of alcoholism. Many of us had done everything possible to make it more difficult for the alcoholic. It's little wonder, to me, that once they had found deliverance and hope in AA, they wanted no part of any non-alcoholic, non-understanding spouse laying an interfering finger on his life-saving program.

It took years for us to gain the respect and support of many AA members and groups. Bill helped enormously; he never spoke without a mention of the help families could get from Al-Anon. He always said it was, "The best thing to happen since AA itself began."

In the beginning we worked only one day a week. The room was big enough for several years, but at first we had little to work with. One long table gave space for opening mail and for Anne's bookkeeping. The ancient typewriter in the small office belonged to AA and was impossible to use. Anne and I used to bring our portables back and forth, which was a nuisance, but at least we could make the keys go down. There was a card table where we ate our lunch and a small table for my machine.

Larry established himself at one side of the room under a large skylight which opened on chains. He could shut it easily, but when he wasn't there the rest of us struggled manfully. As I said, he was an artist but he only worked at commercial jobs when he felt like it or perhaps needed money. For weeks, he'd sit there under the skylight, quietly painting. He seldom spoke but was always helpful. It was good to have him there because it was a long way down those steep stairs and along the half-block hallway to the door.

Frequently some drunk would be waiting, knowing it was an AA clubhouse and he'd be looking for a soft touch for more supplies, not knowing the club didn't open until late afternoon. Oftentimes it was the Coca-Cola man, with cases and cases of Coke to fill the machine and store in the kitchen. That always took time because he'd stop to hunt up all the empties he could find. We'd have to wait until he finished and made out a bill to leave for Larry.

Many times AA's from out of town would stop by wanting to see the oldest AA clubhouse in the world, and we would have to stop to show them around. Everything was alright when several of us were there, but it was uncomfortable if any of us was there alone. I suppose it would have been simple to ignore the doorbell, but we felt an obligation to answer it and were sorry when we found an active drunk on the other side.

Larry knew just where the stops were that would hold the skylight open, and he had magic influence over the janitor who fixed the furnace. We were poor in those days, but we saw to it that we always paid something for rent. The AA group that rented the building would gladly have let us use the space for nothing, but we were following AA policies rigidly. As we grew a bit more prosperous, we'd raise our contribution. We practiced rigid economics; when we finally got enough literature to let groups buy it, Lois brought in Bill's shirt boards to stiffen the packages. The rest of us salvaged strong brown paper for wrapping and we were string savers with a vengeance. Letter postage was then three cents an ounce and it was the one item we couldn't chisel but, somehow, we always had enough for it.

Lois has never quite believed I'm not exaggerating when I speak of a Wednesday between Christmas and New Year's. It was an awful winter, holiday time and everything, and Dorothy and I said we'd get the mail and go to the Clearing House to take care of everything so that people wouldn't be a week late getting answers. We always tried to answer everything the day the letters came in.

We arrived to find the room colder than outside, and a raw damp pervaded the room. We opened the mail; Dot set about making entries of contributions from some of the groups, and I tried to type answers. Gloves didn't tend toward much accuracy and as we got colder and colder we called the janitor more and more frequently. Each time he assured us we'd have heat in five minutes. Larry wasn't there and we didn't know where to reach him. The end came when I tried to sign a spotty looking letter and the ink had frozen in the pen—pre-ballpoint days, of course. We gave up then and went home and worked in comfort.

Larry could control that janitor in person, but never could make him understand we had a right to be there and were entitled to heat. He considered us to be interlopers he could ignore with impunity.

The previous summer had been as hot as the winter was cold. Two very small windows faced across the room from the skylight so there should have been cross-ventilation. There wasn't. The roof was low and tin—had it been connected for solar energy it could have lit up the neighborhood for miles. Larry could do nothing about it. There was a fan, wholly inadequate for half the space.

We would sit, growing more uncomfortable as the day progressed until I expected there'd be puddles of perspiration under each chair. Always, I've been able to bear things a little more easily if I could think up an ugly enough name for them, so I came up with "Lois's Sweat Shop."

Lois always meant Al-Anon to me; I never formally asked her to be my sponsor—we didn't even have them usually. But that's what I've always considered her to be and she still is Al-Anon personified so she got the onus of the heat, and "Lois's Sweat Shop" stuck for the rest of the summer. The day my pen froze I changed it grumpily to "Lois's Ice Box."

For five or six months four of us worked there weekly, with a fifth, Irma, who came in the afternoon. She worked mornings at the AA Intergroup office but was faithfulness itself in devoting the afternoon to Al-Anon.

As Lois, Anne, Dorothy, and Irma spoke to wives of alcoholics they knew, and told them of what we were doing, more groups were established. When I first came to the Clearing House, there were only six groups, as I remember, in the metropolitan area. I don't have the old "Black Book" so I can't be sure and sometimes our entries were not as specific as they might be.

Lois and Anne's group was in Bedford Hills, Dorothy's was the 85th Street Group at Park Avenue, Irma and Sue's group was in Jamaica, and Wally S.'s group was in New Rochelle. There was also a group in one of the Oranges in New Jersey, but not a volunteer from there for some time. The sixth I've completely forgotten. Sorry, and my apologies.

Wally's was an interesting story. His son was an alcoholic, not too much interested in changing in the beginning, but Wally attended every AA meeting he could. He read the Big Book, studied the program, and became so involved in AA that his son's group made him an actual member and frequently took him along as part of their speaking teams. Through Lois and Bill he became interested in Al-Anon and was very helpful. He couldn't be a regular volunteer as he had business responsibilities but was always glad to be called on when we needed new cabinets or shelving. He could always get them for us advantageously.

Sue was another with a full-time job, selling small office machines, supplies, and I don't know what else. She'd drop in frequently, always interested, always full of ideas and usually turned up most magically when we were about to run out of mimeograph paper. Off she'd go and return shortly with a good supply of what we needed.

With all of them plugging the Clearing House—and what a joy it was to work there—others came trickling in. Bill's sister, Helen, was among the first; Wanda from New Jersey; Eleanor, Mag, Evelyn, Clara, Henrietta, Holly, and I don't know how many others.

I had told Lois in that first call that I was looking for a regular job. Our daughter was away at college and I wanted to be out of the house—it was lonesome without her, knowing she wouldn't be coming in from school at four o'clock. I'd stay, I told Lois, until I found one I liked. . . .

I so loved working at the Clearing House I completely stopped looking for a regular job. Then the offer with *The Forum* was so inviting and came so out of the blue I couldn't refuse. But neither could I sever connections with Family Group work. By that time we had established a rough outline of an organization. Our original way of work was that whenever a decision had to be made or a plan worked out, we had a kind of "New England Town Meeting." Whoever was there that day working had a voice in the discussion and when we reached a decision, Lois wrote to the groups to get their acceptance or refusal.

Groups increased. We soon felt we needed a wider basis and more points of view to consider. So we established a regular Advisory Board and invited representatives from several groups not represented by volunteers. Since I couldn't do the regular job and still work at the Clearing House, I asked to remain on the board, which I did.

Eventually it became necessary to incorporate because directors had fiscal responsibility. This bothered some groups. They felt Family Group work would be endangered by organization. I never understood that idea. Incorporation, with good by-laws to follow, seemed as necessary to me as a planned menu for dinner.

Groups continued to grow—to me, like wildfire—but naturally not as they are springing up today. When we answered cries for help, we were happy to find a group sometimes two hundred miles away to refer people to. But I sometimes missed the old, informal town meetings when our monthly board meetings lasted until eleven or twelve o'clock....

We made several moves during those years, always thinking space would be adequate for ten to fifteen years to come. Then we'd find after three or four we needed another two or three rooms, half or a whole floor more. I saw our new offices today and was most impressed. They truly reflect the marvelous growth of Al-Anon in the years I have been away—the result of our really great staff, the blessing of our heaven-sent delegates, and our dedicated, unequalled volunteers.

As I said, I was most impressed by the new offices this afternoon, but it would not surprise me at all if the conference of 1983 or '84 finds them bulging at the seams, perhaps looking for larger quarters. The conference establishment was the greatest thing we ever did. From that first one in 1961 of only twelve delegates, each has left a more solid foundation behind it, a wider vision of needs and how best to supply them. Each has stimulated greater growth and wider recognition of Al-Anon Family Groups.[2] ⤙

IF EVER ONE WAS USED as an instrument for God's work, it was Margaret.

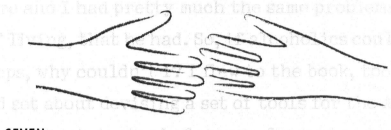

SEVEN

Articles from the *AA Grapevine*

During the decade of the 1940s, Alcoholics Anonymous began to receive a lot of favorable press throughout the United States and Canada. Groups began springing up all over, but along with the new groups a host of new problems loomed over AA's rapidly growing society.

The major tool for communication between the AA fellowship and the foundation office (now known as Alcoholics Anonymous World Services, or AAWS) was the newly formed *Grapevine*, AA's meeting in print. In 1946, Bill W. drafted what became the Twelve Traditions. They were first presented to the fellowship by Bill in the April issue of the *Grapevine*.

After four years of hard work and some compromise between Bill W. and several of the AA pioneers, the Traditions were adopted by the fellowship and became a permanent part of AA. This historic event took place in Cleveland at the First AA International

Convention held in late July 1950. The convention was also where AA's co-founder, Dr. Bob, gave his farewell message to the members. He died later that same year.

Several years before this, both Bill W. and Dr. Bob recognized that it would be unfair for the AA membership to look to them as the future leadership. They felt AA needed an annual conference made up of delegates from each state and province who could represent the membership.

What does this have to do with Al-Anon? As Bill W. traveled the country visiting AA groups and promoting the need for a "General Service Conference," he also saw the need for an organized fellowship for AA families. Lois W., the cofounder of Al-Anon, told this story in Dallas in 1973.

....

Bill got another idea. He thought that AA should have a conference of delegates so that the management of AA affairs could be in AA's hands. So he took a trip around the country by himself; it must have been in '49. When I say "by himself," I mean I didn't go with him. He went to get a sense of the feeling of the groups around the country about having a conference of delegates. He traveled all through the United States and Canada, and to his surprise he found several groups of the wives of AA and they invited him to their meetings.

This was quite a surprise; he hadn't realized there were so many and these had developed spontaneously. They had developed the way I had developed, by realizing that I needed the Twelve Steps. And they had developed perhaps, some, because Annie and I had told them about it—about our experience. And some of them were just what we later called coffee and cake groups. Their organization, if you want to call it that, was to just help AA hang curtains in the club and make the coffee and things of that sort. They didn't have any spiritual program of their own.

When Bill came back from this trip, he took me aside and

he told me that the families of alcoholics needed a fellowship similar to AA that could have a central office people could write to and find out about it. A place where desperate wives could write, and groups could find out about other groups; a central office that could bring these groups into some sort of unity.

So he asked me if I would start such a thing; and, to be perfectly honest with you, I didn't want to. I'd been with Bill through so much in the early days of AA and we had just recently moved to the country to a house of our own, which we hadn't ever had before, and I wanted to work in my garden and make slipcovers for the sofa.

I didn't want to take the time; I felt I had done my job. But once he convinced me of it and I started, I became wholly absorbed and did the best I could. Anne B. started the Al-Anon office with me—the Al-Anon central office. We called it the Clearing House then. We wrote to AA and to our surprise quite a number of wives had written the AA office wanting to be registered. Well the AA office is a place that only registers alcoholics—they didn't have any facilities for registering families.

So we said that we would like to have those names and we would register them. That was just fine with them so they gave us eighty-seven names of people who had written in to the AA office about help for the families. So we wrote to these eighty-seven names and fifty of them said, "Yes," that they would like to join a fellowship of the families of alcoholics.

So that really was the beginning of Al-Anon, but it was really Bill's idea to begin with. And I think if more AA's realized it was his idea, they would be more enthusiastic about Al-Anon.[1] ⤙

AS PREVIOUSLY MENTIONED, the Family Groups started springing up throughout the country using various names. The July 1950 *Grapevine* stated that the first Family Group began in Long Beach, California, on March 1, 1945. But that date may not be definitive. The following article, written by a Family Group member, appeared in the *Grapevine* the previous year, in July 1944. (This *Grapevine* article was written before the AA Traditions had been adopted; some of the issues raised here were later resolved by these Traditions.)

POINTS OF VIEW

Dear Grapevine:

Those who think a wife's troubles are over when her husband joins A.A., just don't know! As an alcoholic's wife, I'd like to tell you. My husband, for instance, still stays out until all hours. True, he's holding another alcoholic's head instead of a bottle—but he still neglects his family even though the bills are paid on the first of the month. He still has his ups and downs and fits of depression, even though they don't last as long and he now recognizes them for what they are worth. In short, our life together didn't automatically smooth out into a placid lily pond just because he sobered up. Not all at once. Where once our troubles made the breach between us an ever-widening chasm, now each difficulty draws us closer together. Of course that didn't happen overnight. When my husband first joined A.A., it seemed as if he were being taken further away from me than ever. And by perfect strangers, too. Even though both of us had been badly hurt by the disease of alcoholism, he was the only one who was "improving." *He* was getting something out of his new associations—*I* was left out in the cold. I couldn't even be a member. The words "sympathetic understanding" were beginning to make me seethe. Why shouldn't I, who had borne the brunt in the past, rate a little of that commodity? Was I always to be left out, first through his drinking, then paradoxically enough, through his drying up?

Suddenly, one day, I had a revelation. Take the alcohol out of the picture and I had pretty much the same problems, of character and of living, that he had. So, if alcoholics could have their twelve steps, why couldn't I? I flew to the book, took pencil and paper, and set about devising a set of tools for the A.A.A.s (Auxiliary A.A.s). Next, instead of my usual morning wallow in self-pity, I began to put my plan into action. I started, like any A.A., honestly looking for my own faults, instead of concentrating on my husband's.

Almost immediately, the miracle began to happen! The sympathetic understanding, which I thought lacking, was there. It had been there all the time, while I turned my back and sought it in another direction. For the first time in years, Harmony entered our front door, not as a polite caller, but as a permanent resident. All this happened, not because my husband had stopped drinking and had gone through a personality change, but because I went through a personality change too. And, although our problems were not always the same, we were now attacking them with the same set of tools. They worked! That's why I'm passing on my personal twelve steps, hoping they may help another through the trying period of readjustment. They are:

1. I admitted that I was powerless to help my husband with his alcoholic problem. (Very bruising to the pride, but humility is easier to live with.)
2. I came to believe that a Power greater than myself could help both of us with our several problems.
3. I made a decision to turn my will and my life over to God, as I understood Him.
4. I made a searching and fearless moral inventory of myself.
5. I admitted to God, to myself, and to another human being the exact nature of the faults I found and the wrongs these caused.
6. I was entirely ready to have God remove all of these defects of character.
7. I humbly asked Him to remove my shortcomings.
8. I made a list of all the harm I had done, however

unwittingly, and of all the mean and spiteful things
I had deliberately done when I had tried to help and
found I couldn't, or when I was feeling sorry for myself.
9. I made amends wherever possible.
10. I continued to take personal inventory and when I was
wrong, *promptly admitted it.*
11. I sought through prayer and meditation to improve
my conscious contact with God, as I understood Him,
praying only for knowledge of His will for me and the
power to carry that out.
12. Having had a spiritual experience as the result of these
steps *(and one does),* I tried to carry this message to
other A.A.A.s, and to practice these principles in all
my affairs.

— An Anonymous Wife[2]

THE *AA GRAPEVINE* PRINTED several articles in the forties about the
"Auxiliaries." These articles provide a wealth of historical information
regarding the development of the Al-Anon program. This August
1946 article was written by an AA woman—again, before the AA
Traditions were adopted.

EXPRESS YOUR APPRECIATION

If there are more than twenty thousand A.A.s scattered throughout the land, there must be, guessing conservatively, at least
sixty thousand of their relatives. That means 60,000 additional
problems—ours! Our attitudes toward them affect our sobriety,
both in quality and duration. Should we not consider carefully
what those attitudes are, since family is often the most important influence in our lives?

Over here on the right, ladies and gentlemen, you find a

school of A.A.s who mentally tack up a large sign: No Relatives Or Dogs Allowed! And over here on the left, is another group who complain that their relatives take only a long-suffering, skeptical interest in the program. Again, here and there, dotted around the country, are A.A. groups that are actually relative-ridden. Some groups don't even dare to have closed meetings, because relatives object. Some gatherings are attended by more relatives than alcoholics; the wives and husbands come, even if their A.A. is sick or out of townkin, hell-bent on getting well *for* them!

An old-timer recently hazarded a guess that 95 per cent of the relatives had never read the chapter written just for them in our book *Alcoholics Anonymous.* Most of them, however, did not know there was such a chapter; of course a lot of them didn't know there was a book!

URGE READING OF BOOK

Point One might well be, then, to introduce the book and chapter to our own families, and to relatives of those on whom we are doing Twelfth Step work, and *urge them to read it!*

But that is only a starter. If we expect to be happy in our own A.A. life, and want newcomers to make the grade, we must be more understanding of our near-and-dear ones. We are so sick and weak ourselves by the time we reach A.A.; we are so full of physical aches, mental pains, moral sores and spiritual bruises, that it is hard for us to realize that those who have lived through our binges with us are generally neurotic cases, too. At this point, relatives are not their real selves at all, they have lived too long in hourly fear, dashed hopes, privations, humiliations and disgust; they have been the objects too often of drunken revenge, vituperation and betrayal. Justly or not, they have been blamed extravagantly for everything. Is it not natural that they, too, will have to go through a faltering period of recovery and readjustment and recapture of faith?

Certainly, they need sympathetic understanding, too—and

need it badly. And they can come to see, and let us hope, experience, how eleven of the Steps can be adapted to their own benefit. Human nature being what it is, it is not likely they are going to achieve all this alone; they need help as we do.

Sponsors and older members can do a generous service by pointing out these values repeatedly during a newcomer's early months.

The more that our relatives appreciate the program, take an interest in the group, are welcomed among A.A.s, and given a sense of belonging, sharing and helping to further the good work, the less friction, frustration and hindrance each of us will suffer in progress.

Take, for example, the extreme disapproval of so many relatives in regard to our closed meetings. Or consider the resentment many of them feel about the long, intimate twosome A.A. powwows that are a major aid to clarifying our outlook. Naturally, such occasions must seem suspect to relatives left out in the cold. If the situations were reversed, might we not conclude that we and our intimate affairs were being discussed—with no chance given for us to tell our side of the story? Or, according to our imaginations, might not we surmise that these were bull sessions, and sex discussions, and might we not be jolly well articulate about it all? Or, supposing we were long-suffering enough to forbear, wouldn't we feel estranged and self-conscious?

Only by thoroughly understanding that an alcoholic will talk to another alcoholic as to no other human, can our relatives possibly come to tolerate, approve and even encourage meetings and confidential sessions.

And as their complete understanding is necessary on this point, so the solution to a great many of the conflicts that often put relatives on one side of a barbed-wire fence, and members on another, lies in the enlightenment of relatives in the whole A.A. program and all that it implies and entails. We should stress the word "enlightenment," too—and avoid the word "instruction"—for the very righteous, ego-puffing attitude that the word "instruction" causes us often to adopt, is salt in a suffering relative's wounds and detrimental to our own pursuit of humility.

It is said—and rightly—that A.A. is the greatest example of democracy in the world. But don't we risk that ideal if we make and feel a class distinction against normal drinkers or non-drinkers, and find ourselves associating happily with alcoholics only? The luxury of being understood, and of being able to talk freely can wreck us if overdone. As soon as we are able to look out as well as in, we might do well to set ourselves a definite goal, to meet and like *all* our fellows, rich and poor, educated and uneducated, men and women, young and old, bores and charmers, *alcoholic* and *non-alcoholic!* With our slogan of "live and let live," we soon learn to sympathize, to listen patiently, to shrug at the prejudices, the foibles, the eccentricities, of perfectly stranger fellow-drinkers, giving them time to iron out their character snags, helping them to do so when we can, and even examining ourselves exhaustively on a challenged point, to reaffirm or readjust our own views. It stands to reason that it would pay off in spiritual and social growth to give the same tolerance and kind patience to non-A.A.s. All non-A.A.s, but most especially non-A.A. relatives.

RELATIVES CAN BE HELPFUL

There are any number of relatives who would be happy to feel useful and a part of things. Why waste such a source of good works? Why not tap such a powerhouse of constructive effort? We find ourselves with a great work to do—helping other alcoholics—and because we seem ordained by our own suffering to do that work as no one else can, and since it helps us "make amends" to the world we live in to do so, we know the strength and healing help that being useful gives us. No relative who properly understands will want to interfere with or intrude on 12th Step work—it's not his forte. But why can't our folk help with the relatives of our newcomer? And aren't there often a

dozen things to be attended to for a new and perhaps rambunc-
tious prospect—anything from broken ear-phones to be fixed,
irate landladies to be calmed, broken appointments to be explained, trains to be met in place of the drunk—and wouldn't
a surprising lot of relatives be happy and proud to work as co-
partner on some of our cases? Certainly there is more work
to be done than there are A.A.s to do it fully and competently.
What A.A. hasn't wished, at some point, that he had 48 hours in
his day? We have all heard many relatives say, with real humility, that they would gladly be "hewers of wood and drawers of
water"—errand-boys and envelope addressers, if it would help.
And as soon as they learn loyalty to observe the sacredness of
our anonymity, so that they can be trusted, not gossip or spread
information, what mistaken altruists we make of ourselves to
refuse their help!

WHY DEPRIVE THEM OF JOY?

If, however, the feeling persists with an A.A. that relatives must
not be involved in any way directly with our activities, should
this exposure to the joy and strength to be obtained through
direct personal giving of oneself to help another go completely
to waste? A husband or wife, mother, son or daughter might be
encouraged to find another avenue of Good Samaritan practice.
There is too much suffering in the world besides alcoholism for
them not to find an absorbing source of spiritual growth in unselfish aid, with our enthusiastic support.

In some towns, relatives have asked for Relatives' Meetings,
and some of these are successfully under way with one or
two A.A.s speaking briefly, two relatives speaking and a long
question-discussion period.

Many of the old-timers around the country are beginning
to wonder whether further development might not be a great
contribution to happiness and co-operation all around. Why not
groups of relatives, run as sort of auxiliary? They might welcome a list of things to be done from which they could choose

their activities; chief of which might well be to welcome relatives of newcomers and work with them as we work with the alcoholics. There are so many kind things to be done for newcomers AND their families, to bridge them into peace with themselves and ease with the world, all quite aside from the program help which only an alcoholic can give to an alcoholic. There are some groups that put across outings, bowling teams, baseball or softball games successfully. Frequent and smaller get-togethers might be stimulating, helping relatives to know each other.

EXPRESS YOUR APPRECIATION

On the little matter of parties—it might go big if more A.A.s expressed appreciation and praise oftener to those wives of members who are forever giving forth with sandwiches, cookies, cakes and coffee after meetings. We are apt to take so much for granted, and neglect the graciousness that could give a kindly heart joy.

With women A.A. members, the opinion and attitude of relatives are often the keynote of recovery and success. Women are generally more answerable to their relatives, less apt to have freedom of movement and time without disrupting a household. If the woman A.A. is a wife and/or mother, or even a daughter, her comings and goings affect other people. And she, even more than a man, needs the warmth of approval, interest, enthusiasm of those closest to her. Unshared interests do not contribute to a happy relationship or a harmonious household. The understanding of her folks can do much to cement a woman A.A. to her new activities and can certainly add to the quality of her sobriety. Surely, there is little serenity when a woman is trying to readjust her whole mode of living amidst surroundings that are cold, unresponsive and filled with misgiving or even downright disapproval or tinged with ridicule. It would seem wise, therefore, to make a far more concerted effort with the relatives of women A.A.s than any other. A husband greeted, welcomed and treated as an important element in the picture may be an oblique kind of 12th Step work that can well forestall a future slip.

Isn't all of this collateral 12th Step work in its way—certainly, "practicing these principles in all our affairs?" In winning and helping a relative to our way of living, we make a fellow-member's road easier in the program—and we add another happy and enthusiastic propaganda-spreader, which is aiding in educating the public in alcoholism, if nothing else.

> —Grace O.
> Manhattan, New York[3]

THIS NEXT *GRAPEVINE* ARTICLE, published in the April 1952 issue, gives a wonderful look at how fast Al-Anon was growing in its early days.

P.O. BOX 1475
AN ADDRESS BRINGING HOPE AND HELP TO AA FAMILIES

The growing interest in the Al-Anon Family Groups has been most encouraging. We are glad to report that where the Family Groups are well established they are in high favor among AA members. One of the main purposes of these Family Groups is to help the AA by trying to give him or her a stable, peaceful home life. The Family Groups realize that they can best do this if their society and name be separate from but allied to AA. That is why the name "Al-Anon" has been substituted pretty generally over the country for AA Family Group, AA Auxiliary or Associates, or Non-AAs.

The three fold purpose of the Family Groups is:

1. To grow spiritually through living by the 12 Steps of AA.
2. To give encouragement and understanding to the AA in home.
3. To welcome and give comfort to the families of AA.

To ensure their success the Family Groups have adopted a tradition that there should be no gossip, nor complaints about the alcoholic's faults at meetings.

When the family of an alcoholic also tries to live by the 12 Steps of AA and to understand the alcoholic, it is bound to aid the alcoholic's recovery. Many AAs have reported that their home life is greatly improved since their family joined the Family Group. Some alcoholics have come into AA as a result of their mates becoming Family Group Members.

As was stated in the June, 1951 *Grapevine,* a clearinghouse with a P.O. Box in New York City was set up as a unifying and information center for inquiring families of alcoholics. Lois W. and Anne B. of Northern Westchester volunteered to staff it temporarily. They worked in their homes on an average of two days a week from May to January answering letters and sending out literature. Most inquiries are from wives of AAs (with a few husbands sprinkled in), but also from the desperate wife of an alcoholic who is not yet in AA as well as from the AA himself who wants to know how to get a Family Group started in his area. A number of wives have reported that through the Family Group they found much serenity although their husbands had not yet stopped drinking or joined AA.

By January, 1952 the interest in Family Groups had grown sufficiently to consider finding a location in New York City where more volunteers could be trained to do the work until the time should come when the clearinghouse could afford a part-time paid worker. The old 24th Street Club very kindly offered the rooms and equipment for this purpose. Here volunteers from the seven metropolitan area groups meet once a week to carry on the work.

Since the clearinghouse was established in May, the number of Family Groups has more than doubled. There were 87 then, now there are 250 registered and many probably that have not written in. By the way, we would appreciate hearing from any Family Group that has not yet written us! Besides the groups in the U.S. and Canada, there are Family Groups in Glebe, Australia; Capetown, South Africa; and Belfast, Ireland. The voluntary donations that have come into the clearinghouse from groups all over the U.S. and Canada have been most gratifying. But to have a paid part-time worker and to purchase suitable equipment, it will probably be necessary to do as the Alcoholic Foundation does and ask all the Family Groups semiannually for voluntary contributions based on some proportionate standard. This step will have to be taken soon.

The families of AAs are eternally grateful to AA for sobering up their loved ones and for pointing the way for the nonalcoholic as well as for the alcoholic to a life of spiritual growth. For the AA member there is no better insurance for happy sobriety than a contented family that understands. The Al-Anon Family Groups everywhere are trying to bring this about.[4]

IT'S EASY TO SEE that these Family Groups grew quickly in number and in strength as they banded together in unity and purpose. Here's another *Grapevine* article from an AA wife, published in March 1952.

ENCOURAGEMENT FOR NEW MEMBERS' WIVES IN NAA

I am the wife of an ex-drunk and I mean ex, thank goodness, for he has been a member of Alcoholics Anonymous for the past four years. Before this I had many years of worry and unpleasantness caused by his drinking.

Today I have found *my* place also in the Alcoholics Anonymous organization by joining NAA Group, and I am happy to tell how much it has helped me.

After my husband joined AA I was glad to go to meetings with him, and help in any way I could, but I soon learned that this was his program. I read the Twelve Suggested Steps and tried to practice some of the principles and such sayings as "easy does it," "first things first," as well as the prayer which starts *"God grant me the serenity..."* I did get much out of all the meetings, but felt that my husband was getting something more from the program which I needed too, which was fellowship and understanding. This caused me to feel a little left out until I joined NAA Group, and here I found not only fellowship, but the privilege of asking questions as to how best I could help my husband and myself straighten out some of our problems. I discovered that these women and men had some of the same difficulties to overcome as I, and so I was able to profit from the way they had solved their problems.

I learned to be more unselfish by trying to help others, which gave me a feeling of being a part of the program pattern.

We also have our Twelve Steps to live by.

In the group we make many friends, to whom we feel close enough to call on when things are not going too smoothly. But the most important function of NAA is to encourage the wives of *new* AA members. Often they come in confused and desperate, not knowing what it is all about, and never sure whether their husbands are really sincere. They want desperately to understand; but they haven't got used to this new life yet, and it seems impossible that it can be true—they think, in fact, that it must be too good to be true.

Once they have been made to see more clearly how they can help at home they begin to have a glimmer of hope—hope that perhaps they *can* be a real help through understanding and patience.

Above all we must take an active role if we want to grow with our husbands, and thereby gain more understanding and peace of mind.

If you have a NAA Group, attend the meetings as often as possible.

—Mrs. C. J.
Miami, Fl[5]

AS MENTIONED PREVIOUSLY, Al-Anon Family Groups were able to avoid many of the pitfalls that the early AA groups experienced. This is perhaps because the "wives" were so involved with AA in its infancy that they were able to learn from those experiences and apply them in their own fellowship. These early Al-Anon groups laid a strong foundation for the success this worldwide fellowship has enjoyed for the past six decades and continues to enjoy today.

EIGHT

Messages from AA's Cofounder
to the Family Groups

Many Al-Anon pioneers recognized that perhaps their movement's greatest supporter and cheerleader was Alcoholics Anonymous cofounder Bill W. Not only did Bill stand by his wife with constant support, encouragement, and love, he also reached out to the suffering families of alcoholics throughout his life, with deep concern for their well-being.

Over the years, Bill W. counseled many alcoholics who were suffering from broken homes and irreconcilable marriages. Not all alcoholics were as fortunate as he to have a wife who stood by during the most difficult times. Many lost their spouses and families—never to have them return.

Bill worked tirelessly with alcoholics and their families, wanting to help them in any way he could. He was often bothered by just how little time he had to spend with Lois. Sometimes they would simply take off for the weekend, just to be together. When he was speaking at AA and Al-Anon meetings, he would say that the alcoholics, when first sober, would find themselves "married to AA." Perhaps this was a confession as to how he felt during his early sobriety.

There is little doubt that both Bill and Lois felt challenged at times by the demands placed on them by their respective fellowships. During the 1940s and even through the mid-fifties, while Bill was authoring both the AA Traditions and the World Services structure, which became AA's second and third legacies, he suffered terribly with periods of depression. In a 1959 correspondence to his doctor, he reflected on these bouts, saying, "I managed to largely conceal the situation, although it was frequently suicidal in content."[1] Lois stuck it out with him and did all she could to help Bill during these very difficult times. It was obvious they were deeply in love with each other.

It's interesting to note that when Bill wrote the book *AA Comes of Age*, published in 1957, he had just come out of nearly fifteen years of depression. Perhaps the term "depression" in some way suggests a debilitating condition—this was far from the truth in Bill's case. During that time he made perhaps his greatest contributions to the recovery movement. In spite of the bouts of depression, he enjoyed many good times with Lois and his AA friends. One could easily assume that these positive results were brought about by his continuing practice of AA's Twelve Steps. Coincidentally, his depression lifted and he started feeling better personally at exactly the same time he turned the AA affairs over to the General Service Conference.

This 1957 letter demonstrates clearly how Lois felt about their marriage after having spent thirty-nine years together. It was written on their wedding anniversary.

. . . .

Bill, my darling,

Today starts our 40th year together. As the years have piled up, my respect, admiration, and love for you, dear, have risen and broadened and deepened until now all my girlish ideals of mar-

riage and married love have come alive and are being fulfilled.
We are companions, friends, and lovers.
   Thank you, darling, for this wonderful gift of yourself.
         —*I love you,*
         Lois
         1/24/57[2]

ON THE SAME DAY, Bill presented Lois with this anniversary message.

• • • • • • • • • • • •

January 24, 1957
Dearest Lois,
   Thank you for this year gone past and all that went before. No
one could have had your sustaining courage that saw me through
the night. None could have been a friend, partner in the glorious
day which God has granted us.
   I shall love you, dear, forever.
         —*I Love You,*
         Bill[3]

AS MENTIONED IN CHAPTER SEVEN, Bill W. traveled extensively in the
late 1940s and early 1950s throughout the United States and Canada.
During his trips, he was often invited to attend Family Group meetings and on one particular occasion he spoke to a large gathering of
non-alcoholics, mostly AA wives, in Salt Lake City. The following has
been transcribed from that June 1951 talk.

When we alcoholics are permitted at such meetings, I think
the first thought that crosses our mind is this: "Where in God's
heaven did we ever find such a wonderful, loyal bunch of
people? These drunks really must have something to attract
folks like you. That goes very much for the Wilson household,
like many another alcoholic, since I'm one of those who would

not be alive had it not been for a wife who stuck. She stuck to the very end, which was almost the bitter end. She stayed in that dark cave with me when all others had gone. So without her, I doubt very much if I would have survived.

She was the one who brought me to the place where I might receive the message when it came—so it has been with uncounted thousands of us. So my first and joyous duty is to record the debt of gratitude that we drunks owe you, dear people, those ones so near who saw us through. Then comes AA; the drunk revives; he sees the light! He becomes ecstatic; and then the poor wife who had a problem on her hands of a drinking drunk suddenly discovers that she has on her hands the problem of a dried-up drunk, which can be, as you know, quite a problem.

For the bad boy, the problem child now comes in the front door all charged up with spirituality and he says, "Momma, you had better get a load of this, and by the way, Momma, where is the pocketbook; where is that checkbook?" And he lets her know right away that he has become the head of the household. Well of course, Momma, overjoyed, scarcely notices that at the time. Although she does, in her quiet moments, wonder just how it was that with all her devotion and love the man didn't get sober, and, instead, the local plumber did the job where she failed. It's a hard one to take, isn't it?

Then it appears this [AA] is something exclusive. This "drunk club" is something in which they belong, but you don't quite belong. In fact, they have these "alcoholic-only" meetings. Some places don't have *any* open meetings and then it's AA morning, noon, and night.

The house is full of talk about AA; the house is full of drunks both sober and intoxicated. Everything has to stand aside and wait unless it's a matter of AA. And if you say anything to the newly converted drunk, he says, "But, Momma, this is Alcoholics Anonymous. You want me to stay sober; these things have to be done to maintain my sobriety."

So then you don't see him evening after evening. He's out

there in that drunk club. And then you begin to feel like a hen who has hatched a duck egg and the damn duck is now on the pond. He's over around the point there with his other ducks, and will that duck be home for dinner? Well you don't know, maybe. Then you reflect that around the corner with the male ducks there are also some female ducks of the alcoholic kind, too, and you fear there may be competition.

So life among the anonymous, for the wife as she goes along, isn't always too easy. Well, back in the early days of AA, the first few wives who came in quickly perceived this new situation. They felt something ought to be done about it. In the first AA club down there on 24th Street in New York, we had an upper floor. And it was supposed by some of the wives that they—and a husband or two who had gone along with an alcoholic wife (of course those fellas are really rare)—would have a meeting up there all by themselves while the AAs were having their very exclusive meeting downstairs.

When that was proposed, there were murmurs; there were anguished protests. The alcoholics downstairs said, "We wonder what is going on up there. My wife already has too much on me. When these women put their heads together, what are they going to have on all of us?" And, "Won't those meetings generate into a sort of gossip meeting?"

Well, those early meetings were called for the purpose of getting a better understanding of the alcoholic—as though you didn't understand pretty well already. They did kind of degenerate, and I heard there was some gossip; however, that's not peculiar to the wives of the alcoholics. So the thing sort of bogged down. That, however, did not mean that the wives of alcoholics didn't continue to serve Alcoholics Anonymous.

As I have so often said about Lois—working in the department store daytimes, and coming home to cook for a house full of drunks at night—she did all the work and I took the bows. And that's about the way that the wives of us drunks have been going along ever since. Coffee and cake for those fellows out in the front room, and nursing that drunk in there while your husband is off to work—smoothing the way for this thing, trying to adjust things with the kids. Yes, this has been your lot.

I don't think it's been as happy as it might have been if we drunks had been more thoughtful. Now then, in the past few years a development has taken place in separate places; women in twos and threes—occasionally with the husband participating—that thing has begun to flower into what we now call AA Associates or AA Family Groups. Here, as in the very early times, the wives and the husbands of alcoholic people are getting together in definite meetings, but this time with a very different program.

This time with the realization, as your preamble so well states, that the drinking in all those years has distorted you and has distorted the whole family relationship. So then, we are no longer meeting to understand the drunks—we are now meeting to understand what has happened to us, with the realization that in many cases we have become the man's mother. That the whole family relationship has been distorted, and what can we do about this by applying those same Twelve Steps to us? Then, it's not only a matter of applying those Twelve Steps to us, but what can we do for that new wife coming in, wondering if her husband can get sober, or the wife that comes and says, "He won't even look at Alcoholics Anonymous, but I need to understand this situation."

So here we now have the Family Group, which proposes to have its own meetings, and sometimes very exclusive meetings, I might add. I was amused the other day while in Los Angeles when an alcoholic came up to me rather indignantly and said, "You know, my wife is an alcoholic, and you'd think she would talk to me; but as a wife she's entitled to go to these family meetings. So she goes to those damn family meetings and, you know, they're so secret she won't even tell me what goes on there."

"Well," I said, "you can be comforted because practically all these family meetings have a rule, that only the problems of the family are to be discussed. The drunks are not to be discussed or gossiped about," and such is this very promising development that's going on.

Down at the Foundation office, we have a record of some eighty-seven Family or Associate Groups. I suppose that means there are 187 of them around. In parts of the country where this development has flowered and has paid off in much-improved domestic relations, the drunks are going for it in a big way. Up in Toronto, for example, where the Family Groups have been very effective, no alcoholic thinks of setting up an open meeting without picking as one of his speakers a member of the Family Group. One speaker out of every four or five is a Family Group member. If you were to propose such a thing in other parts of the country—if I were to propose it even—I think the drunks would excommunicate me. They're so scared of these women getting together.

But this is a growing thing and it's a fact of AA life and it is certainly one that Lois and I welcome and she sends her regrets that she can't be here to share this happy hour with you. Now, your question is, "Where do we go from here? Where are we going to be placed in Alcoholics Anonymous—way out in the lot somewhere behind the barn? Or are these Family Groups to be called AA groups; or are they to occupy some intermediate position?"

Well, the debate on that subject has already started among the drunks and some of them have expressed these fears; if these Family Groups are permitted to operate as groups, we're confusing the whole purpose of Alcoholics Anonymous. AA is dedicated to one sole purpose—that is to helping that drunk get sober. Therefore, if we go into the Family Group business, why pretty soon we'll be trying to save the whole world and it may divert AA from its main purpose.

So a lot of drunks still don't like the idea. They're skeptical; therefore, AA as a whole can't yet declare any particular policy.

But as I remind these fearful drunks: "What's the use of arguing? The Family Groups are already a fact of AA life. It isn't a question, my friend, of whether you're going to have Family Groups; you've got 'em! It's only a question of what the status is going to be and how they're going to operate for their best interest and the best interest of AA as a whole. And my friend, as for your fear, we have come to realize that alcoholism is a family problem. When things are fixed up in the family circle, the chances of recovery for the drunk are very much improved.

So therefore, these Family Groups do have a bearing on AA's single purpose to help the other alcoholic recover if he wishes. So it's largely a question of status. And now the foundation has been laid with all of these inquiries from existing Family Groups and would-be Family Groups. The question was put to the conference which met in New York last April, though it was only half-size to be sure: "What shall be the status of these Family Groups?"

The conference isn't as yet able to speak for AA as a whole; they were only half-size and it was their first meeting. Quite properly, they didn't try to define any status and may not try to define any status for several years.

But they began to think it over, and those who had come from sections where the Family Groups were a red-hot growing concern got up and spoke to the others who were doubtful about it. So I think this thing can go on evolving very nicely, just as it is, perhaps with this much central aid.

It may be that when the status of the Family Groups is finally decided that they will wind up with a department down at the foundation and maybe a group directory; and maybe a pamphlet or many pamphlets and maybe a book and means of communication. It's too early yet to make such a move; I'm not even suggesting such a move. But in the meanwhile, it seems to some of us, including Lois, that we ought to at least establish communication with these groups around the country.

So it was suggested that she and a temporary committee of

AA gal neighbors take out a post office box there in New York, right near the foundation box. And let it be known around the country that there was such box for inter-communications; a place where questionnaires could be circulated to find out how things are getting along and what the main problems are, to create sort of a nominal center. Actually, this development is not as far advanced in New York as it is right here in this room, as a matter of fact.

The only reason we suggested New York for the post office box is because, if at a future time we did want to have a department for you folks in the foundation, it would be very inconvenient to have the department in Salt Lake or San Francisco. It would be very hard then to tie it to the foundation, so for that reason, a post office box to establish communication has been gotten. I'm hopeful that the *Grapevine* will presently publish more pieces on this wonderful development, and will give you the number of that box and that all will prosper. And meanwhile, Lois carries you—her deep thanks and her deep love to which I add my own.[4]

BILL STAYED VERY BUSY with his AA work in the early fifties and understood that Al-Anon needed to stay separate from AA. Of course, he would help out whenever summoned, but he seemed very comfortable allowing Al-Anon to establish its own identity. Margaret D., the editor of *The Forum* and a Clearing House staff member, said, "When we came to something needing a decision where we had no experience, Lois would say, 'Let's ask Bill.' He would be out sitting on the floor or lying on the table, but would immediately offer his help by sharing the AA experience with us."[5]

Bill and Lois were invited to speak at the Texas State Convention in June 1954. Bill was excited about this trip because his sponsor, Ebby, who had relapsed, was now sober in Texas. This would be his first opportunity to thank his Texas friends for helping Ebby and would also allow him time for a visit with Ebby.

Lois did not join Bill on this trip because she was still recovering from a heart attack she had had on their thirty-sixth wedding anniversary. Lois was scheduled to speak to the Family Group members at the convention; since she was unable, Bill filled in for her. Here is what Bill had to say.

· · · · · · · · · · · · ·

Well, I came in here to pinch-hit for Lois and no alcoholic, let alone me, could possibly do such a job. As you know, she is a symbol of all of you. You will want to know about her health. The attack wasn't bad; it's getting better, though she can't withstand the rate of activity she used to. But she sends you all her warmest love and is really desolate she can't be here.

If you will bear with me a couple of minutes, I would like to review what has happened since the beginning, with respect to you who have stuck by us in our caves where no others would come until we saw the light. After years I now realize that the part you played in this thing has been infinitely more difficult than the part of the alcoholic. Your suffering you had to take standing up and you had to take it sober; and in a sense your difficulties and suffering had not stopped just because we drunks had sobered up.

Lois so often tells how overjoyed she was when Ebby, my friend, came along and precipitated the experience that set me free. Then Lois began to realize that this new thing had come into my life and that where before I had been her sole and rather fragile, dubious possession, I had been all hers. Then she realized that I was becoming the possession of other people, too, and that realization was a little tough to take I'm sure, and must be for all of you. As this thing grew, the gal became, as many of you have, sort of an AA grass-widow. In my case I think, psychologically speaking, the bride became Alcoholics Anonymous.

So we drunks, me included, went about taking the bows, and you people plodded on doing the work, carrying the responsibilities, still making all these things possible. Now it is only in recent years that we have realized what an immense dislocation this can produce in the family. Not only on the surface, but underneath and often invisible.

Because of our drinking, we force you people to become our parents instead of our partners; very often we force you to become head of the house. We force you to go out to work; we force you to become the mothers and nurses of bad boys and in some cases the non-alcoholic husbands of very bad girls. So, there was a profound psychological dislocation that took place, through no fault of yours. As I now see it, I can't imagine a more blameless lot of people than you were. Anytime that a drunk complains to me about how his wife is his mother or about how she nags him still, or how she tries to run his business, I say, "Listen mister, you were the guy that made her this way."

Well, some of this began to appear quite early in AA. As I said, Lois had her first pangs and then she compensated for the fact that the honeymoon didn't resume immediately by beginning to take alcoholics into the house, where we just ran a laboratory on drunks for years. And then as the group grew, down our way, and it was the same in Akron and Cleveland, of course, you began to come to open meetings. Of course you began to exchange experiences, but still, even back then, I'm sure that many of you didn't feel like you quite belonged. You found that these drunks were sort of exclusive, sort of snobbish, sort of patronizing. They would have the nerve, after batting you around for years, to say, "Momma, I've got the Twelve Steps—what about it for you?"

Well, that's a pretty tough dose to take when you lavish love on a man for years. When you feel, and often rightly, that you are more to him than anyone else, but still you can't cure this thing: alcoholism. So up comes the local plumber with his overalls still on, and in thirty minutes flat he's got this guy started on the way to a cure that you couldn't do in thirty years.

Now I submit that is an ungodly, merciless deflation and the manner in which you people have taken it has been superb. As time wore on, of course, in half the cases there was a wonderful family reconciliation, family reunion, life began to go on at last. You people saw that the drunk would have to get married to AA if he were to stay sober and, in half the cases, after a while things worked around alright.

But in the others there was still this mysterious lag for which nobody could account—why didn't the honeymoon start again? Why was it that we couldn't turn the clock back plenty before all these terrible things started? In later years, we have been getting wise as to why that is, and as we have gotten wise, both alcoholics and you, dear partners of ours, have begun to see the remedy. In fact, you have begun to use the remedy yourselves.

It is quite useless and would be really futile for an alcoholic to go home and say, "Look, you've got to be my mother. I love you as my mother, but not as my wife. Now why don't you change over?" We can't say those things to you. We who have been so much at fault—no, but you can say these things to each other.

Now in the early Family Groups there was some conversation of this sort. There was also a good deal of conversation on how to understand the alcoholic—very important. There was also conversation on how to manage the alcoholic better. In one of the revisions that you folks made of the Twelve Steps, the First Step was changed to read: "We found ourselves powerless over our alcoholic husband."

In your distress and your desire to inform the new ones coming in, you have begun to band yourselves together in these Family or Associate Groups. And now, instead of asking, "What is alcoholism?"—as you've asked for years—you're asking, "What has this drinking problem done to me? I who have done the best I can; nevertheless, I'm very much in the wrong because without even knowing it I've gotten distorted. So what did this thing do to me? What did it do to our children?"

Now you ask those questions of yourself and you take the

Twelve Steps for yourselves and you begin to do Twelve Step works with the incoming wife or husband of an alcoholic.

When you came to that conclusion, these Associate Groups and Family Groups began to spring up like wonderful flower beds everywhere. The movement has grown so fast that in the last three or four years the number has jumped from like seventy to something like seven hundred. Characteristically, the alcoholics were heard to say, in many quarters, "Well, now here come these gals again, they're going to butt into our exclusive club, and divert AA away from its main purpose and all sorts of terrible things are going to happen."

But the more thoughtful ones of us knew better than this; we could see that this was to be the beginning of a movement within a movement, which might indeed one day become larger and greater and more powerful than even AA itself. Because what this movement promotes is not alcoholic sobriety, what this movement spells for you and your family and for many people in the world outside is emotional sobriety.

As you looked inward and you appropriated the Twelve Steps to yourselves, as you made your own inventories, as you made your restitution, as you did your Twelve Step work—well at that point you ceased being and you commenced to belong in a sense that you have always wanted to. Your place in this thing became established. I personally think that this is one of the greatest things to have happened to AA, almost since the beginning.

Now, as I said, about four years ago the Foundation began to get listings of Family Groups and there were all kinds of Family Groups going under many different names. There were many versions of the Twelve Steps. This movement, just starting as such, was beginning to get publicity. Where would the inquiries go? Who would form a suitable literature for it?

These same questions came to us about the Foundation fourteen years ago. It was very obvious there had to be some organization to it. So I asked Lois, already overburdened, if she would sort of front this thing for a little while until it could have a service center, a directory, something similar to the Foundation. It later could be taken over by you in the way that the AA services are run.

Well, the literature is under way and you've decided to adopt the Twelve Steps and the Traditions with slight variations. Inquiries are flowing in and national publicity is beginning to appear. The inquiries are being distributed, group problems are being solved by retelling of information, and so the benign process is well under way and at a prodigious rate.

So I think that, speaking for the drunks, we can do much more than to welcome you to AA meetings. We can now say to you, "Girls, you've joined up and we're damn glad!"[6] ⌐o

IN THE MID-1980S, I had the privilege of getting to know one of the Texas Al-Anon pioneers quite well. Arbutus O. was the first delegate from Texas to Al-Anon and the only one to have the distinction of representing the entire state. She went on to become one of Al-Anon's trustees. As noted earlier, much of the archive I have today belonged to Arbutus and her husband, Bill.

I recall visiting with Arbutus one evening and asking about her relationship with Lois and Bill. She immediately said, "Well, I would never consider myself to be a close personal friend of Lois."[7] This was perhaps her attempt at humility, because certainly the letters exchanged between the two and the "gifts" from Lois to both Arbutus and her husband found in the archives would lead to the conclusion that they were close friends.

I continued to ask questions and specifically asked her about Bill W's relationship with Al-Anon. She said, "He was always a gentleman; he would arrive at the Al-Anon World Conference early and put flowers at Lois's place for her. He opened his home to all the Al-Anons and was always willing to answer questions. He was our biggest supporter and was so grateful for all the good that had come from Al-Anon."[8]

On another night Arbutus told me of the first time she met Lois W. She said, "It was the night before the first trial Al-Anon World Service

Conference and I was sitting off by myself drinking a cup of tea. I was very nervous being in a big city and I was scheduled to speak the next morning. A little lady came over to the table and asked if she might join me; she was Lois W.

"I welcomed her and told her that I was nervous and apprehensive about speaking the next day. Lois just smiled and said, 'You'll do fine, Arbutus. Just speak so the newest member can understand every word you say.'"[9]

It's funny looking back on these times with Arbutus, because she had become a very popular convention speaker. And she always spoke so that the newest member would understand every word she had to say. I believe Lois gave her great advice.

While at that first World Conference in 1961, Arbutus had the opportunity to hear and meet Bill W. It's obvious that Bill was very proud of the growth and accomplishments of the Family Groups. He shared these words with the Al-Anon staff and delegates:

> *Growth-wise, as a movement, you have exceeded anything that ever happened to AA in its early days. And this is, we all know, because you have been intent on filling the vast vacuum that has long existed in family relations. We alcoholics, on getting sober, were quickly able to get back to some sort of job. Now there is a little money in the bank, and we are madly active in AA. We make restitution to everybody in the world except the people we have really mauled, and those people are your good selves.*[10]

His speech continued by sharing AA's experiences with the delegates present. He believed that the "Trial World Service Conference" would prove to be a permanent and important part of Al-Anon, just as it had become for AA. His closing remarks to the conference were:

> *May God bless and keep you all. May He set His special favor upon this auspicious beginning. You will surely look back upon this day as a great one in the annals of the Al-Anon Family Groups.*[11]

When listening to the many speeches that Bill W. gave to Al-Anon Family Groups over the years, there's little wonder as to why he received so many invitations to return. His willingness to share the learning experiences of AA with the Family Groups was admirable.

Many times he spoke as if he were a member of Al-Anon. Having experienced alcoholism in his own family as a youngster, he undoubtedly would have qualified as an Al-Anon. He had a deep understanding of alcoholism at various levels and degrees and knew intimately the devastation it can cause each family.

As Bill got older and his health began to fail, he was not able to accept as many speaking engagements. His schedule narrowed to just a couple speeches per year during the last few years of his life. The last recording I could locate of Bill speaking to the Al-Anon Family Groups was at a meeting following the WSO (World Service Conference) in April 1968. His health was not good; nevertheless, he was able to make an outstanding talk that lasted thirty minutes. This may have been the last recording of Bill addressing the Al-Anons. The theme of his talk was "World Services," and I believe it is fitting to conclude this chapter of messages from Bill with his closing remarks from this conference.

. . . .

In AA, and I'm sure in Al-Anon, the advice is oft given, "Live in today; yesterday is gone; tomorrow is not here." This is great advice because obviously the fellow who is still trying to live in the past is either living there with his guilt, or the memory of superficially joyous days that he would like to reenact. He is so preoccupied with this thing that he stultifies his own growth and is a drag on people about him. In the best sense of the word, he is an "ultraconservative"—he fights change; he lives in the past.

Then we have people who are "over-living in the now," you might say. Their main chance being in the next hour; so they flutter from this, to that, to the other thing. Being so preoccupied by the "now," they cannot learn from the experiences of the past and drag it into the "now" for use; and this is the function of the Traditions. Neither are they able to think about the future— maybe because they are afraid—so they dwell in the "present" and not necessarily with any great or successful growth.

Then we have the people who are the dreamers. We'll always

need a certain number, but obviously one cannot emotionally live in the future. Because of the realities of today, they can't operate in the framework of now. These are the liabilities that we come to when we divide time into the past, present, and future.

But look at time in another way. Is it not, with us humans, a stream of consciousness on which we are borne along from the past, into the present, and into tomorrow? And therefore, I think that we must more consciously, while always refusing to live emotionally in the past or emotionally in the future, be ready to get a sense of history as to the experience of yesterday, so as to keep those Traditions infused with the power to guide and protect us today.

And should we not give thought for tomorrow? Not in any fearful sense, but in a sense of prudence and responsibility. Where are we going as individuals and as a society, toward better things? Are we settling for complacency? Are we crying for spaceflights? What are we doing, and is it sound? Will it spell progress for tomorrow?

Well, in the happy state in which we find ourselves in this year of our Lord 1968, all this happiness, all this wonder, all these miracles can bring us complacence. But let me pose what some of the problems of the future might be: religious schism? No, probably never; the ecumenical spirit of the world, in its solidly uniting front, crossing all religions does away with that possibility that might have arisen even a hundred years ago here and elsewhere. No, but in the world today, have you ever thought what would happen if AA had to go underground—if our people occasionally faced firing squads? I say this not in fear, but just in prudence. Let us remember our blessings; let us take right thought for the lessons of yesterday that they may bear upon today and tomorrow, and tomorrow, and tomorrow, for as many of them as God would let us have.

Good night, and God bless you.[12] ⤳

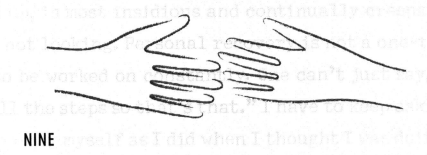

NINE

"We Need This for Ourselves":
The Story of Lois W.

Condensing Lois W.'s story into one chapter for this book seemed, at first, to be an insurmountable undertaking. However, I am fortunate to have access to many audio recordings of Lois throughout her life. And through the kindness of Annah Perch, I have had the opportunity to research the archives at Stepping Stones. My goal is to offer an accurate and concise story of this amazing lady.

I have attempted to minimize the details of the more commonly known aspects of her life and share some lesser-known information. The following accounts are based completely on Lois's own words from both letters and audio talks, with limited author comments.

••••••••••••••

When Bill and I were first married we, of course, were terribly happy. But before that, when we were engaged, he never took a drop to drink. His father had too much to drink most of his life, and his grandfather before him, and he saw the results. His mother and father were separated mostly because of alcohol and he had been warned that he should never take a drink because something awful might happen. And somehow or another he had believed them, and I was very proud of him. When we were engaged I told people how wonderful he was because he'd go to the saloons (as they called them in those days) with the boys and drink ginger ale, or sarsaparilla, or root beer, or some other drink of the time.

He was stationed at Ft. Rodham, Massachusetts, which was a cotton manufacturing town and there were lots of well-to-do socialites there. The men, of course, were all gone to war, but the women put on cocktail parties for the men at the post. It was at one of those parties that Bill first took a drink of liquor. I used to like to kid him and tell him that he couldn't resist the women—he resisted the men when they offered him a beer—but he couldn't resist the gals when they offered him a cocktail.

The first time I went to a party with him in New Bedford, Massachusetts, "the boys" came to me and said, "We have just taken Bill home and put him to bed." So I immediately went home, and there he was with a bucket at his head.

Bill drank till he was laid-out every time. It wasn't too often, and although I was shocked about it, I was sure that I could fix him. I didn't think it would be long before living with me would be so stimulating that he wouldn't need any artificial stimulant. But, year after year went by and he got worse and worse. And as we had no children, it became my one purpose in life to help Bill get over this frightful "habit" as I thought it was. But nothing seemed to work; we tried all kinds of things and he was so remorseful and so anxious to stop this drinking that I never could be too harsh with him, the morning after. I always had to say, "Well, better luck next time, you'll do it next time." But next time came and the same thing happened again and again.

We got into the outdoors, into the open air, and went on picnics or camping trips, or hikes through the countryside, which Bill loved. He never drank during those times, or very very rarely. So, we would have our wonderful weekends together and would do all kinds of silly things sometimes, depending upon how much we had in the pocketbook.

We would take a row boat and put up a bath towel on an oar and sail up the Hudson River. I remember one time we did that and camped on a spit that came out from Nyack, New York, on the Jersey side. But the mosquitoes were so bad that we couldn't sleep; so we got back in the row boat and put our blankets on the floor and anchored out in the channel where there was a good breeze, to keep the mosquitoes away. But the great vessels that were going up and down the Hudson River, kept honking, beeping their horns at us, and we had a very precarious night, there on the Hudson, amidst all of the big traffic.

When Bill first came home from overseas, he really didn't know what he wanted to do. He hadn't had any profession when he went into the Army during the war, so he didn't know what he was going to do to make his life work. We decided we would take a month or so off and we put packs on our backs and we walked across Maine, New Hampshire, and Vermont trying to decide just what he'd do. Of course we had a wonderful trip, but he wasn't any surer when we got home, than he was when he started.

So, there were lots of wonderful and companionable times that we had together in spite of the great unhappiness that we both felt because of his drinking. He sincerely and earnestly wanted to stop and couldn't. He wrote in the Bible, way back in 1928, "I promise you, my dear wife, never to take another drink." And he truly meant it, I believe.

His drinking got so that he was good for nothing, absolutely nothing, but drinking. He would stay home while I went to work and I had to make all the decisions. Even though the years went on and we went through some very difficult, hard times, I would have rather been with him drunk than away from him.[1] ∽

LOIS FOUND GREAT COMFORT in writing, drawing, and doodling. In 1928, she wrote a several-page document, which is in the archive at Stepping Stones, under the title of "Outpouring." It is obvious from this document that Bill's drinking had become very serious and Lois had found herself confused, frightened, and filled with despair. The following excerpts are from that document.

· · · · · · · · · · · · · ·

Does love make the world go round? Can a person, by loving with all her heart and keeping faith in the ultimate victory of good over evil, eventually win out after failure after failure? Is it worthwhile trying or is it simply knocking one's head against a stone wall and nothing but silly, maudlin sentiment? What is one to think or do after so many failures? Is my theory of the helpfulness of love and faith that I have held to so long nothing but bunkum? Is it better to love and hope and fail than lose the companionship of striving together and the consequent zest this gives to life in spite of the depressing failures? Is it best to recognize life as a series of failures and one's husband a weak, spineless creature never going to get well or is it better to gloss these over with a thick coating of hope and love, repeating and repeating that love will win out and ultimate victory will be attained, dwelling on the good characteristics only of one's mate, of which there are so many?

Perhaps I take the whole thing too seriously and that it is nothing much that one's husband is dead drunk three nights out of the week when we are in the city.

If, I should lose my love and faith, what then? As I see it nothing but emptiness, bickering, and taunts and selfishness, each one trying to get as much out of the other as possible in order to try to forget the lost ideals.

I'm writing down all this confused medley of ideas and half ideas in order to help me think my problem out, which is this—

I love my husband more than words can tell. He is a splendid, fine man—in fact an unusual man with qualities that could make him reach the top. His personality is, I think, what I love most; everybody loves him and he is a born leader. I had practical evidence of this during the war. He is the most kindly, bighearted soul and would give away his last sou. When he is drunk he is so penitent and self-derogatory and sweet that it takes the wind out of your sails. He is honest almost to a fault, except that once or twice he has lied to me about his drinking, but always has confessed later of his own free will. He has a delightful, whimsical sense of humor and an unusual vocabulary, employing unique phrases so that he is an interesting talker. He is an impelling one as well, for in every gathering people listen to him intently. He has an unusual fund of knowledge because of his remarkably retentive memory. His mind is the far-seeing, long-perspective kind. Minute details bore him to death. He once had a bookkeeper's job and nearly expired and his books and hands and desk were blotted with ink. He is extremely careless about many things and never knows which pocket his matches or keys are in. Around the house I am forever picking up after him; but that is a trivial matter. In several notable instances he has tackled something hard and never given up until he has accomplished it. If his interest is aroused there are no ends to which he won't go. And yet he is a drunkard and cannot apparently get over it. We have been trying almost daily for five years and it is worse now than before. If we go away on a trip he says he does not miss it and will go without it a month at a time; but the minute we get back to the city, the very first day, in spite of all kinds of plans and protestations, he is at it again. Sometimes he will come home fairly early and sometimes 5 o'clock in the morning but he always comes home. I should have said above, among his outstanding, fine characteristics are his faithfulness to me and his lack of interest in any other woman, as such. This I am as sure of as a person can be of anything. We have been so close and honest with each other for these ten years that there can be no doubt of it. . . .

After all these pages where am I? Have I made anything

clearer? I don't know—but I do know that I love my husband and that I am going to have faith in the ultimate success of our struggle, that I am going to appeal to the good in him and keep on everlastingly trying.[2] ⤚

IN 1929, Lois did leave Bill for a short period of time. She wrote the following letter to Bill while she was away in Washington, D.C. It clearly shows how devastating Bill's alcoholism had become and just how desperate Lois was.

· · · · · · · · · · · · · ·

My darling,

I love you so, I love you, I love you, I love you. God grant that I am doing right in going away from you. I can barely bring myself to do it. (Try to make it easier for Mother while I am away. This is going to be a terrible shock to her.) Fight for me, my sunlight, my darling little boy that I held in my arms and sang to the other night to help him. I won't say that it all was in vain. It was just the first step towards victory that we fought together. These next steps are going to be still harder and dear one you are going to have to take them alone, not spiritually alone, but physically alone, for I'll be with you every single minute in love and thought. Bring me back to you just the first moment possible. 7 days without a touch of liquor.

You better go up to Holyoke. It will be easier for you there. Understand darling I'm doing this to help you. I don't know whether it is right or wrong. I only know that it is one of the things I haven't tried that may be a help. I'll prove it so dear heart. Billy dear, no matter what I do to help or hinder, Honey, the fight is really up to you in the end. Don't be so terribly discouraged by this last failure. As it goes in golf, "It's the next stroke you're going to play, not the last one that counts." And I'll be with you in spirit, rocking you in my arms and singing to you. Don't forget that dear when it's hard. I wish I could be near you when you come to tomorrow morning.

Think about me every second of the time dear and how anx-
ious I am to come home to you. Don't keep me away from you
long. Let's go away together someplace soon after I return. The
other night was the beginning of the real victory I am sure dear. I
love you, I love you, forever and ever and ever.
　　　　—I love you,
　　　　Lois[3]

AFTER THE STOCK MARKET CRASH in 1929, Bill was able to secure a job through a friend in Montreal. The Wilsons were able to live in comfort for awhile, until Bill's drinking progressed, while his hopes for controlling it diminished. Upon returning to New York, Lois and Bill moved into her family's home on Clinton Street with her father. (Lois's mother died on Christmas Day 1930.) Lois took a course in interior decoration at the New York School of Fine and Applied Art while Bill was able to get a job (that didn't last) with Standard Statistics.

Lois later took a job selling furniture at Macy's Department Store. While working there, she submitted an article on veneers to Condé Nast Publications for which she was paid seventy-five dollars.

In 1933, Bill was admitted to Towns Hospital for the first time, to help him quit drinking. He returned two more times, with December 1934 being his last visit.

Here's a note Lois found when she arrived home one afternoon.

• • • • • • • • • • • • •

December 11, 1934
Dear Lois—
　　I think I said that if matters approached a crisis—the inevitable
result of the first drink—I should go to Towns. I am going there.
　　I also said that under no condition would I go to Towns. I shall
not try to resolve these inconsistencies. On the one hand is the
great pressure, on the other the promise of a new fine life. I shall
not delay a moment.
　　　　—Yours, you do not know how dearly.
　　　　Bill[4]

AFTER READING BILL'S NOTE, Lois wrote one to herself: "I found this when I returned from work and was hurt and sore that he hadn't consulted me about going to Towns and I was paying most of the bills and he had been there only a few months before." [5]

It is apparent from these notes that Bill had made yet another promise to Lois to not incur additional expenses in his quest for sobriety—he had already failed twice. But this visit to Towns Hospital was different. Several weeks earlier, his friend Ebby had stopped by Bill's home. Ebby, once a hopeless alcoholic, had been sober for two months. He gave Bill great hope.

Ebby came to visit Bill in the hospital. Bill spoke of that day in the book *Alcoholics Anonymous.*

> *My schoolmate visited me, and I fully acquainted him with my problems and deficiencies. We made a list of people I had hurt or toward whom I felt resentment. I expressed my entire willingness to approach these individuals, admitting my wrong. Never was I to be critical of them. I was to right all such matters to the utmost of my ability.*
>
> *I was to test my thinking by the new God-consciousness within. Common sense would thus become uncommon sense. I was to sit quietly when in doubt, asking only for direction and strength to meet my problems as He would have me. Never was I to pray for myself, except as my requests bore on my usefulness to others. Then only might I expect to receive. But that would be in great measure.*
>
> *My friend promised when these things were done I would enter upon a new relationship with my Creator; that I would have the elements of a way of living which answered all my problems. Belief in the power of God, plus enough willingness, honesty and humility to establish and maintain the new order of things, were the essential requirements.*
>
> *Simple, but not easy; a price had to be paid. It meant destruction of self-centeredness. I must turn in all things to the Father of Light who presides over us all.*
>
> *These were revolutionary and drastic proposals, but the moment I fully accepted them, the effect was electric. There was a sense of victory, followed by such a peace and serenity as I had never known. There was utter confidence. I felt lifted up, as though the*

great clean wind of a mountain top blew through and through. God comes to most men gradually, but His impact on me was sudden and profound.[6]

Lois later spoke about that day.

. . . .

And when finally, that marvelous thing happened to him that probably most of you have read about in the Big Book *[Alcoholics Anonymous]* when he had this wonderful spiritual awakening, I knew right off that he was a different person; that something tremendous had happened to him and I never had any doubts from then on about Bill's drinking. I knew that was a thing of the past and I can't express to you my gratitude for this wonderful thing that happened to him.

He'd had this wonderful experience; he knew he was sober and was going to stay sober. Why couldn't this beautiful thing happen to others? Why couldn't it, in fact, happen to all the drunks in the world? And I think he must have brought nearly half of those drunks home to Clinton Street, because we had the house full of drunks in all stages of sobriety and non-sobriety. We had many ridiculous experiences, many, many inspiring experiences, and some tragedies there.

We had a rule that nobody could come in the house when he was drinking. So one of the boys we wouldn't let in opened the coal chute and got into the cellar. I was surprised that he could, because he was quite large, but somehow he was able to slide down the coal chute and got in that way. The same big man got stuck one night in the basement wash tub—he decided to take a bath but couldn't get out. I believe it was me who had to pull him out. Another man committed suicide in our house after having pawned our clothes.

So then, when Bill sobered up, and he didn't need me anymore, I couldn't understand it. I at first didn't let myself believe that I was unhappy. I thought, I rationalized, I was quite sure that after all these years and he'd finally gotten sober, that I must be happy. I was sure that I was happy, but I didn't know where I fit into the picture anymore. I was still working for quite awhile and had to work. That part, I was needed in, and I had to get the meals for a number of these drunks as well as ourselves at the house. But I didn't feel the spiritual need that I had before.

I think I'll tell you a little bit about how Bill came to have this spiritual awakening. An old friend of his came to him. This friend had been a terrific drinker; a very, very heavy drinker and he came to him and he was sober. Bill said, "Well, what's got into you?"

And this boy Ebby said, "I got religion."

Well Bill was shocked at that idea of getting religion. He had become quite atheistic and he just didn't understand and then Ebby, who had been helped by some friends at the Oxford Group, explained the principles of the Oxford Group. You admit that you are powerless over your life; that your life has become unmanageable; and you ask the help of God, of somebody greater than yourself to help you. Then you take your own inventory and see where you have failed and you try to make amends to the people that you have hurt. There were six of these principles that were used by the Oxford Group.

Well, we went to the meetings of the Oxford Group; I went along, like any good wife should with her husband, but I didn't go for my own sake, I went for his sake. I had never dreamt that I needed any Oxford Group or any religious program. I'd had a good spiritual bringing up. I had a most loving family and I had all the answers; I didn't need, even though I hadn't accomplished what I'd set out to do, which was cure old Bill of alcoholism. Yet it never occurred to me that it was me—well, it did occur to me that it was my fault. Lots of times I wondered what I was doing wrong, but I did also believe that nobody else could have done it; that I had the right principles, it was just something in Bill's illness (and I did think he was ill because I knew that he was such a fine person). It must be something beyond his control because he had shown willpower before and control of things.

So, one day Bill said to me, "Let's hurry and get ready and go to the meeting."

I had a shoe in my hand and I took that shoe and threw it just as hard as I could and I said, "Damn your old meetings."

I wasn't a person who was given very much to swearing. And I was flabbergasted with myself afterwards. I couldn't see what it was that had gotten into me. Why had I reacted so violently to such a simple remark of his? What was it? What was bothering me? What was eating me, as they say?

This surprised me, I think, more than it did Bill. I didn't know—I wouldn't let myself think that I was upset at all. But until this moment, I hadn't thought about myself in relation to Bill, and to man, and to my God. I had taken myself for granted. I had been brought up in a good, religious home and I'd had loving parents, and it never occurred to me that I hadn't behaved as a good wife should. I'd done all I could; I wanted so to be helpful and, as I say, I'd thought that I was on the credit side of the ledger and that Bill had been on the debit side.

I just never stopped to analyze myself at all, and when I did, after this shoe-throwing episode, it just started me to think and to wonder about my own behavior and my own attitudes. I began to really get down to brass tacks with myself and I realized that I was resentful about these new-found friends that Bill had; that I was jealous of Ebby, who had come to Bill and sobered him up.

I had tried to sober Bill up for about seventeen years and I hadn't been able to do it and here's somebody that had come along and in a few minutes—a few minutes talk with Bill, and Bill was somebody completely different. And I had really been very, very much hurt by this. So I went along again to these meetings, not just because Bill was going, which had been my motive previously, but because I needed to go; because I needed spiritual development. I finally woke up to that fact.

This started me thinking about my own attitudes and actions. Previously I had just taken them for granted, because I knew that my intentions were good. It had never occurred to me that was not enough; besides relatives and friends had continually told me that I deserved great credit for putting up with so much, both during the drinking and after. Sometimes I believed them. And sometimes the knowledge that I had failed at my life's undertaking—at sobering up Bill—made me very remorseful.

Bill had started drinking just before we were married. And, unfortunately, as we then felt, we had no children. My whole life's effort for seventeen years was to help Bill overcome his destructive habit. Regardless of the difference in temperament and upbringing, our standards and interests were similar. We were very close despite alcohol's disrupting influence. He tried very hard to stop during his last few years of his drinking and together we did everything we could think of to help him. When we were first married, I had no doubt that life with me would soon straighten Bill out.

As the years of drinking stretched on and on, I'm sure my so-called patience with him contained large parts of pride and stubbornness, as well as the deep love I had for him. After the shoe-throwing episode, I took the Oxford precepts of self-analysis more seriously and began to change my smug attitude about being such a good influence on my husband.

As AA evolved I applied its principles to myself. But it took me many years and continued soul-searching to fully realize how much harm my self-righteousness had done to both Bill and myself. Self-righteousness, unlike alcoholism, which cannot be covered up, is most insidious and continually creeps back when you are not looking. Personal recovery is not a one-time thing; it has to be worked on constantly. One can't just say, "Now I've taken all the Steps so that's that." I have to keep asking whether I'm fooling myself as I did when I thought I was doing the best I could to help Bill stop drinking.

True, I know much more about myself now, but it is so easy to rationalize where one's ego is concerned. I have to be constantly on the alert. Sometimes seemingly unselfish acts have deep self-serving motivation, which is hard to detect. On the other hand, feeling remorseful and guilty for doing the best one can is not only useless, but harmful. So I try to hit a happy medium: not to either fool myself about my motives or blame myself for the past. Length of time in Al-Anon teaches much, but it never bestows a diploma.

When Bill was out in Akron on this business job that fizzled, and he met Bob Smith, he stayed there for a large part of the summer. I was working, and when my vacation came, Anne Smith invited me to come out and stay with them. So I took a bus and rode out to Akron.

Anne and Bob were most gracious in their acceptance of Bill's wife. Anne was a remarkable woman; she had a lot of very deep wisdom. She couldn't see very well, so she liked to sit in a dark corner, and she smoked incessantly—a chain smoker. Where she got all her wisdom from I never knew, but later on AA's and families of alcoholics all would come to her, and sit with her in her dark corner while she would help them out of whatever problem they happened to be mixed up in at the moment. We really had a wonderful two weeks together, and then I had to come back, and get to work again.

Anne had belonged to the Oxford Group—Anne and Bob both—as had Bill and I before AA. But Anne had taken it very much more seriously than I had. I had felt superior; I felt that I didn't need the discipline of the Oxford Group. And therefore, my recognition, finally, that I did need the Twelve Steps, and that I did need to change my way of living, was really more drastic than I believe Anne's was because she had already been practicing and living a selfless life.

There was no way of communication except going places when AA was first started. We used to go everywhere. Bill would be downstairs talking with the AA's, which were mostly at that time men (there were very few AA women in the early days); the wives upstairs would meet with me. We would be playing bridge or doing something or other, but I would tell them a little bit about my experience and how I had come to realize that I too had to live by the Twelve Steps. That when I did realize that, everything became so much easier and happier at home.[7] ⚬

LOIS WROTE THE FOLLOWING LETTER in 1950 on their anniversary. It clearly indicates that she was attempting to live by the Twelve Step principles.

• • • • • • • • • • • • •

January 24, 1950
Bill darling:
Another year has passed and I feel that it has been, particularly the latter half, one of progress for us both. I can't tell you how relieved and happy I am that you have emerged from the suffering of the "black night." It may be some counter-balance to the pain for you to know that it seems to me, never has the bright day shone so brightly. We have a deeper understanding of each other and ourselves and so much more consideration for the other fellow's point of view.

It seems after these 32 years together that we have really learned how to live a partnership. Darling, you make me happy in so many ways and I am proud and grateful to be your wife.

The flare-up that I had this summer was caused by nothing but self-pity and hurt ego, I'm convinced, and I'm going to try to be on my guard never to let such an accumulation of acid drip down into my subconscious again.

You know I have a theory about subconscious reaction. I believe that up to a point the conscious has control over it and all its primitive instincts. Mother, for instance, loved so truly and wholly that there was no residue of the acid of resentment and self-pity to drip down into the subconscious and arouse the primitive

instincts. Mother most certainly had them the same as you and
I, but these weeds were never watered by the conscious so were
kept in a dormant state and never had the opportunity to poke
their shoots up into the conscious.

What I mean by "up to a point control of the subconscious" is
that these primitive instinct weeds are very virile. If we can, like
mother, wholly love, they remain forever dormant. But we so often
fool ourselves into thinking we have no self-pity or resentment,
but a few acid drops at a time are seeping down to water and fer-
tilize. These primitive weeds quickly grow to maturity and when
they do there is not much control over them. The control is in not
watering them. What I believe is done only in one way—by love—
love of husband, or wife, of family, of fellow man, and love of God.

Dear Bill, after 32 years of loving you I am asking God to
teach me how to love more completely.

> *—I love you, dear one.*
>
> *Lois*[8]

IN THE FOLLOWING TALK, Lois shared the history of the beginning of
Al-Anon.

•••••••••••••

Little groups of wives and families all over the country began
to feel the same need. They needed something for themselves
to help them to stop being the frustrated people they were, and
to be real, integrated human beings. So that's really the way
that Al-Anon started. We followed AA in every possible way we
really could.

Bill and I had been so very companionable; we had lost all
of our friends. We had nobody but each other and then, all of
a sudden, the house was full of drunks. He went to Akron and
he met Bob, and AA really started at that time. And it went on
and on; it kept growing and many exciting things happened.
The book was written, the AA book, and the AA conference was

formed. The Traditions were written and then back in 1950, I guess it was, Bill was interested to find out what the AA groups felt about a conference of delegates.

Bill felt that the AA's themselves should have the say over their own affairs, so he went out to all the groups to get their opinion and to see how they reacted to the idea of a conference of delegates. And when he came back, he told me about his experiences and he said, "You know, there were a whole lot of groups of the families of alcoholics and I think something should be done with them." He suggested that I start a fellowship, an office for the families of alcoholics—a place where they could write for information, where they could meet other AA's or Al-Anon's.

We had been quite surprised and disappointed in the early days of AA to find that the families were not as happy as they should be, after this wonderful program had come to the alcoholic. We thought everything should be simply marvelous in the home, but it wasn't. There was something missing and, of course, it was that the family was not going along too—were not living the same program.

So, I asked a friend of mine if she would help me. It was another Anne, Anne B., this time, to help me start the office for the families of alcoholics. Of course, we didn't know what to call it, but we made up the name Al-Anon from Alcoholics Anonymous and sent out a questionnaire asking the groups whether they would like to use that name and whether they would like to use the Twelve Steps of AA as principles to live by.

We got from AA, to our surprise, eighty-seven names of people that had called up, or written to the AA office, for information about the families of alcoholics. And AA was not equipped to send out any information about the families; they were only equipped to deal with alcoholics. So they just kept these names; they had answered the letters politely, but that was all they could do. So there were eighty-seven names when Anne and I asked them to send us any names they had, and we wrote to them all. We got fifty answers, which I think was really a very good percentage.

Al-Anon really started with fifty groups, and then Anne and I asked them about the name, as I say, and about the principles and they wrote back and said, "Of course they'd like to live by the AA principles. Then Anne and I got so busy that we couldn't keep up with our work up in Bedford Hills, where I lived. She used to come and help me there. So we moved to New York and the AA's offered their upstairs room in the clubhouse on 24th Street. The first clubhouse in the world, by the way, and we started our little Al-Anon office there and we got in a lot of volunteers.

We went around, Anne and I, and the father of an alcoholic, Wally. There were maybe about five or six groups in the New York area at that time and we went there and asked for delegates for our service office. And we had five or six really dedicated people that came in. We only met once a week, at first, and then we had to come twice a week. Then we had to get a regular paid secretary and Henrietta was the one chosen, and she's been there ever since.

Al-Anon got started and has grown at a simply remarkable speed; of course it had AA to break the path, cut the brush, and so the trail was very much easier to follow. But nevertheless, we feel that it's been just remarkable. It took the application of the Twelve Steps of AA for us to really see a lot of the things about ourselves. Alcoholism is so obvious that it is very easy to see when a person has had a slip, but with us wives and husbands of alcoholics, we've been put in the position of being on the right side of the ledger. It isn't obvious that there is anything wrong with us.

I'd always thought of myself as being the moral mentor in the house. Bill never was a mentor, but he was certainly growing spiritually while I was standing still. I don't really believe there is any "standing still." If I wasn't going ahead, I was going backwards. So I decided I had better live by the Twelve Steps too. In our meetings we tell our own experiences just as AA's do. We tell how we came to find that we needed Al-Anon and what Al-Anon has done for us, and we sought to help other families that had the same sort of experience.

I think it is so much harder for us to apply the Twelve Steps. I think one of the biggest problems with us is that we are not honest ourselves. I'm talking about myself; I'm putting it in the plural because I suppose it applies to a lot of us; but I know it was hard to be honest with myself and see why I did this and why I did the other and not make myself think that it was from some fine purpose and not just because I was selfish. So, Al-Anon has come to be, for me, a completely new way of life. And I hope I am getting more honest myself, but I think that really is the hardest thing of all to be.[9] ⌒

AT FIRST, Lois wasn't excited about heading up this new Al-Anon fellowship. She was thrilled to finally have a nice home where she could garden and enjoy activities she had been unable to do, both during Bill's drinking and the early days of AA. However, it seems that she brought just the right amount of dedication and love to Al-Anon to see it through its infancy.

Borrowing from AA's experience, Al-Anon adopted its own version of the Traditions and the Twelve Concepts. In 1961, the organization held an experimental World Service Conference that evolved into an annual event in 1963.

Bill and Lois traveled extensively throughout the fifties and sixties, sometimes for weeks at a time. A seven-page document entitled "Record of Dates" in the Stepping Stones Archives is almost entirely devoted to documenting Lois's travels from 1925 to 1983. It's interesting to note that from 1950 until Bill's death in 1971 the couple traveled together over forty times with a dozen of those trips outside the United States.

After Bill's death, Lois picked right back up and headed out in early 1972 for a "world tour" with her friend Evelyn. She continued to travel throughout the remainder of her life. The same records show that she made thirty additional trips between 1972 and 1983. Many of these were related to Al-Anon and AA functions held in various parts of the world.

Lois had a love for children that lasted throughout her life. She was very aware of how alcoholism affected them. In a talk she said, "The children were so vitally interested in everything that went on. They would inquire about all the people and wanted to know how they were. They learned the Twelve Steps and were themselves really trying to live by them."[10]

In 1986, at age ninety-five, Lois received the Margaret Cork Award from the National Association for Children of Alcoholics. This award, which is given annually, honors individuals making contributions in the field of children of alcoholics.

Lois was unable to attend the presentation; however, she did send a written message. In her letter, Lois provided some historical information about Alateen. She wrote, "I would like to thank the National Association for Children of Alcoholics for honoring me with the Margaret Cork Award, in recognition of the part I played in the incorporation of Alateen into Al-Anon Family Groups."[11]

Lois went on to say that as early as 1954 Alateen had begun to surface. At the 1955 St. Louis AA Convention, there were speeches entitled "Children of Alcoholics" that discussed problems young people had to deal with in the home.

After the convention, the Al-Anon Board began plans to release a publication based on the talks given in St. Louis. It became Alateen's first piece of literature printed for the national market.

Lois went on to clarify that the name "Alateen" was adopted in June 1957, which was six years after the founding of Clearing House. Two of the first three recognized groups for children of alcoholics were in California while the third was in Durban, South Africa.

"By December of 1957, there had been a total of fifty-three inquiries about Alateen," Lois continued. "Ten new groups had been registered, including two in Vancouver, B.C., and one in New Zealand; and the decision had been made to include sample copies of *Youth and the Alcoholic Parent* with all Al-Anon literature orders."[12]

Lois concluded her message by downplaying her role in the development of Alateen, instead crediting Al-Anon Family Groups. I believe Lois considered her role to be closer to that of a grandparent toward a child, rather than a parent. The award is currently displayed at Al-Anon Family Group Headquarters in Virginia Beach, Virginia.

Lois's contribution to the entire recovery movement is beyond measure. It is conceivable that without her love and support neither AA nor Al-Anon would have begun, not to mention the many other Twelve Step programs that have sprung up. Today, untold numbers of beneficiaries throughout the world live by the Twelve Steps and enjoy a sense of well-being as a result of her pioneering efforts.

Lois passed away on October 5, 1988, at the age of ninety-seven. She is survived by the millions of AA, Al-Anon, and Alateen members whose lives have been forever altered as a result of her acceptance and willingness to recognize that "we need this for ourselves."

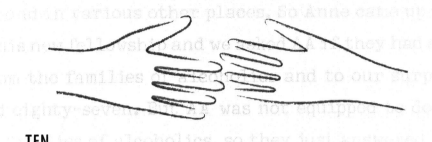

TEN

The Story of Anne B.:
Cofounder of Al-Anon

This is the story of Al-Anon cofounder Anne B., from Chappaqua, New York. Anne's husband, Devoe, owned and operated Chappaqua Motors, a successful auto dealership and service center. They sold and serviced various makes of cars, including the luxury vehicles Cadillac and Rolls-Royce. Devoe didn't start drinking until after he and Anne were married, and it wasn't long before his alcoholism became a serious problem. As Devoe's drinking problem increased, Anne had to help out at the dealership while caring for their two daughters.

At one point, Anne was so desperate she left her husband and children for a short time to seek a divorce. But she returned home without following through with her plan. Their family doctor suggested she call a man who might be able to help Devoe with his drinking problem. Anne made the call and met a man from AA who gave her a pamphlet. At that time, AA had only one pamphlet; it was made up of a series of articles written by Larry J., which had first appeared in the *Houston Press*. Anne left the pamphlet on a table in their home, and the next day Devoe cried out for help.

I was unable to determine exactly when Devoe started attending AA, but it was most likely early in 1941. He attended meetings with Bill W. and another friend from Chappaqua, Tom P.[1] As these early AA members joined together for fellowship, their wives also began to grow close through their common bond as wives of alcoholics. Throughout the entire decade of the 1940s, Devoe struggled with his sobriety. He finally achieved complete sobriety in 1950, which lasted until his death in 1960.

Anne and Lois met in 1942, not long after the Wilsons moved into their Bedford Hills home. They became friends while attending the same open AA meetings with their husbands. The two wives often discussed the principles of AA while waiting for their husbands. During those difficult years while Devoe struggled with his sobriety, Anne continued to attend Family Group meetings while doing her best to raise their two daughters. Later she decided to start a Family Group meeting in her home with Lois's help. The first meeting was attended by fifteen women.

As mentioned earlier, Bill W. spent a tremendous amount of time traveling throughout the United States and Canada. During these trips, Bill met with many of the wives' groups and saw the need for a national headquarters that could help organize these floundering groups of non-alcoholic family members. Upon returning from a trip, Bill prompted Lois to take charge of setting up a clearinghouse. Lois recalled the event in a 1983 recorded talk.

• • • • • • • • • • • • •

When he came back, he said to me, "I think you should start a fellowship, like AA, for the families of alcoholics." And as I said before, I didn't really want to do this, because we hadn't had this house for long and I was so excited about having a house of my own and a garden. I wanted to have all of my time for that and not take it to starting a fellowship. But I began to think about it and I saw how badly such a thing was needed. So, I asked a friend of mine, Anne B. She was in an Al-Anon group—we had several groups, we called them "family groups" in our neighborhood and there were lots of them, as I say, around in various other places. So Anne came up to help me start this new fellowship, and we asked AA if they had any inquiries from the families of alcoholics and to our surprise, they had had eighty-seven. But AA was not equipped to do anything for the families of alcoholics, so they just answered the people politely and told them they would keep their name on record or something, that's all they could do. So they gave us these eighty-seven names and Anne and I wrote to them and asked them if they would like to form a fellowship of the families of alcoholics and to our surprise, fifty of them answered.[2] ⤙

LOIS ASSUMED THE CHAIRMANSHIP for the policy center, with Anne B. as secretary. She was grateful to have Anne's help. Anne had attended a business college and had developed some very useful skills. She went to Stepping Stones each week. Dividing up the workload, Anne and Lois communicated with the new groups. Anne gave the following report in the minutes from a meeting held at Stepping Stones on November 17, 1951.

Last April A.A. held its first General Service Conference in New York, which consisted of Delegates from all over the United States, and many of their wives accompanied them. Lois invited these wives, as well as women from local Family Groups, to her home for a luncheon. There were 40 women in all. At a meeting after the luncheon it was discovered that nearly all the women belonged to a Family Group in their home town. Lois told of the increasingly important part these groups are playing in assisting the alcoholic.[3]

LOIS AND ANNE WORKED two days a week answering inquiries. By May, letters had been sent out to the eighty-seven original inquiries telling them about the Clearing House and giving a contact address: P.O. Box 1475, Grand Central Annex, New York 17, N.Y. An article in the June 1951 issue of *Grapevine* about Clearing House also brought inquiries. In most instances, the letters were pleas for help, questions on how to start a group, or complaints about husbands.

Meeting minutes clearly illustrate just how rapidly Al-Anon was growing with two hundred new groups from May through November. The rapid growth continued and by the close of 1952 Al-Anon had a total of 441 groups worldwide. This certainly was a testament to just how desperate families were for help in dealing with the alcoholic problem.

In 1955, AA held its Second International Convention. The convention, which celebrated the twentieth anniversary of Alcoholics Anonymous, was held in St. Louis the first weekend in July. This historic event also marked the first time the Family Groups met at one of AA's international conventions with the name "Al-Anon Family Groups." The 1950 convention had the participation of the "wives' groups," which, as described earlier, existed before Al-Anon was formally organized.

Each day of the conference, AA issued a bulletin with highlights and program events. In the center of the first bulletin, written in bold letters, was "FAMILY GROUPS MEET." Under this heading was the following:

For the Al-Anon Family Groups, composed of wives, husbands and other relatives of alcoholics, the St. Louis Convention will be historic in more ways than one, Lois W. predicts.

It will mark the first time that the 700 Family Groups throughout the world have held an international meeting with a "formal" agenda. And it will go down in "Al-Anon" history as the time and place when Groups published their first basic textbook, "The Al-Anon Family Groups—A Guide for Families of Problem Drinkers." The attractive, informative handbook will be on sale for the first time in Family Group Headquarters in Kiel Auditorium. It has been in preparation for nearly two years.

Four Family Group open meetings have been scheduled today and tomorrow. Members and friends will have the opportunity to meet a number of Family Group Clearing House staff people.[4]

ONE OF THE AL-ANON MEETINGS held at the convention was the Al-Anon Family Group application of the Twelve Steps. This session had various speakers talking about their personal experiences with the Steps. Anne B. was the last speaker on the program. She was quite nervous and spoke briefly to the large crowd.

Anne began by discussing her acceptance of the First Step when she recognized she was powerless over alcohol. It wasn't until some years later that she began working on the Fourth Step, a "moral inventory." During her quiet time each morning, she wrote her inventory; she did this for several years.

Anne discussed some of her fears and the early experiences she shared with Lois, especially attending the wives' groups and helping Lois set up the Clearing House. Of course, the crowd in St. Louis was excited to meet Anne and to learn of her experiences related to the formation of Al-Anon. She was not introduced as the cofounder of Al-Anon, but was recognized as Lois's first volunteer and the vice president of Al-Anon.

Anne continued her Al-Anon service until Devoe died in 1960. She remarried about a year later, but the marriage ended in divorce after just a short while. She finally settled in California near her daughter and grandchildren. Anne didn't remain active in Al-Anon, although she continued living a spiritual life.

Anne's daughter, Madeline, lived in Santa Paula, California, and in many ways followed in Anne's footsteps. She worked as a secretary in the school district until her retirement. She also volunteered for many organizations, both during and after her retirement. Although not known to be an Al-Anon member, it was apparent that she enjoyed helping others like her mother. Madeline lived until December 2009. (Another daughter is mentioned in a 1983 speech given by Anne, included below.)

Anne did make several appearances at Al-Anon gatherings while living in California. Her last appearance was just months before her death. She was on the program with Lois Wilson at a conference in southern California. Her ability to recall the early Al-Anon events had diminished considerably, and she was only able to talk for a little over five minutes. The following are excerpts from Anne's final talk.

. . . .

I met Lois and Bill in forty-two. I met them at my husband's sponsor's home and you know it's a strange mystery the way he got his sponsor. Our doctor, who didn't know what AA was, said to me, "You go up and see Wilbur." Because I was at my wit's end and I was going to leave, period. Well I went to see Wilbur and it was years after that that I knew that was his last binge too. ⌐

SHE continued:

. . . .

When we first started, we called it the Clearing House. And Lois and I would put out the money to have this literature sent away. Then lo and behold, one day, wouldn't you know, a man from Lynn, Massachusetts, sent us a donation. That was our first donation and after that it really came up very nicely.[5] ⌐

THE INFORMATION AVAILABLE about Anne B. is limited, and for the most part has already been made available through Al-Anon literature. I encourage the reader to investigate additional written information directly through the Al-Anon World Service Office.

I was able to locate just two recordings of Anne's voice and neither detailed much about her personal story. I find it coincidental that both Anne and AA's cofounder, Dr. Bob, were involved in their respective fellowships for fifteen years. Dr. Bob passed away fifteen years after helping Bill W. to found AA, while Anne B.'s life took a new direction after the loss of her first husband. The contribution made by these individuals to their own fellowships was lasting and significant.

It's fitting to end Anne's story with her closing words at this conference, in which she referred to a favorite poem.

....

I want to say a few words . . . in memory of my daughter who died in January because of alcoholism. And these words I think are very appropriate: "I come to you then in love and thought, to tell you that immortality can never be bought. You must come to God in humility and love, and send your heart to him who's just above."[6] ↝

ELEVEN

"I Needed a Meeting Long Before
I Picked Up My First Drunk"

The personal stories in this chapter and in chapter 12 present two instances of Al-Anon in action today: members recounting their own experience with the Al-Anon fellowship. They show that Al-Anon members, made up of men and women who are relatives and friends of alcoholics, solve their common problem through sharing their experience, strength, and hope with others while learning to live by the Al-Anon Twelve Steps. They symbolize the hope found through personal recovery in Al-Anon.

The stories reflect the opinions of the individual members. They do not speak for Al-Anon Family Groups as a whole. They are shared as illustrations of the recovery that can be found through Al-Anon, with the hope that readers who can relate to them might decide to investigate the Al-Anon program for themselves.

The man who tells the story in this chapter has a viewpoint entirely different from that of the woman who speaks in chapter 12. But both stories trace their journeys, sharing what they used to be like, what happened, and what they are like today. Our first speaker is a man named Aaron.[1]

....

For the most part I grew up in an alcoholic free home. The only active drinker was Grandma, and I don't know that she was an alcoholic. I remember her being the fun one. She was the one who allowed me to sip her beer and she occasionally acted inappropriately in public. But she didn't ask me to get dressed up so she could take me to church, like the other adults in my life. I really enjoyed being around her.

Growing up in a religious home in Charlotte, North Carolina, isn't really uncommon. I was the oldest of five children and our home was filled with love. However, it was also filled with fear. All through my childhood I thought those two things went together. Love was intertwined with fear; if you loved someone, you were afraid for them all the time. If you weren't fearful for them, maybe you didn't really love them.

In between having babies of their own, my parents brought in foster kids. Those kids really needed the love my parents provided because most had come from terrible situations and many had come from alcoholic homes. They received unconditional love because they needed it so badly.

It was different for me; I always felt like I had to "perform" for my parents to love me and that just didn't seem fair. I don't know where I got that idea—it certainly didn't come from my parents. Every holiday our dining room was filled with the homeless and "less fortunate" people my mother invited. I knew this was a good thing, but I never saw it that way. I was uncomfortable, frustrated, jealous, and resentful toward my mother and wondered why she thought she needed to save the world.

These early memories show that I developed character defects while very young—although it took many years before

I recognized that these or any of my personal characteristics were anything less than outstanding qualities. At the time I thought these traits were what made me a good person.

As I look back at these events growing up, I see the type of person my mother was; she was always trying to help someone or to fix a problem. I've had time to reflect and to try to understand what it might have been like for her, growing up as the oldest child in a home of a problem drinker. I have come to understand that alcoholism is a family illness, and I experienced it firsthand growing up in an environment influenced by a generation of problem drinking.

I can now see that my mother was very much an untreated adult child of an alcoholic. I want to clarify that I'm not a medical expert, and I've been taught in Al-Anon that it's not my job to classify anyone as alcoholic—I'm simply not qualified to make that diagnosis. I love my grandmother and perhaps she's not an alcoholic; she may simply be a heavy daily drinker. But the effects of her drinking on my mother, in my opinion, were a contributing factor to her emotional instability. I've also heard it said, "If you look like a duck, quack like a duck, and waddle like a duck, you're probably a duck."

As a child I hated almost everything and everyone, including my parents, teachers, and the church. I'm certain that I was taught about a loving God, but as a child I never remembered hearing it. My perception of God was that He was "making a list and checking it twice!" I was already not able to please my parents or myself. I just knew that I'd never be good enough for God. Consequently, I rejected the idea of God very early on, thinking, "If this is what He's all about, I want nothing to do with Him."

As I share my story, I want to emphasize that all these events and circumstances are my own perceptions of things. I have three sisters and a brother who all grew up in the same home, with the same parents, and yet their reactions to life and their emotional instabilities did not become visible the same way mine did.

It sounds cliché to say, "My parents did the best they could with the tools they had." But this really is the truth. My dad was always involved in my life. If I was playing sports, he wouldn't just be there, he'd be helping to coach. I always resented him for this because it was either an embarrassment to have him there or he wasn't doing it my way.

My upbringing and my grandmother's drinking were not the cause of me becoming a member of Al-Anon. I also want to state that it's not as if I was going along in life acting and thinking like a normal person, and then I met an alcoholic. The character defects that make my life unmanageable—self-centered fear, resentment, self-pity, and anger—developed in me very early in life. I don't remember a time when these things didn't rule my life. I needed a meeting long before I picked up my first drunk.

I attended a small, private religious school connected with our church until I was halfway through eighth grade when they asked me not to return. My parents chose to homeschool me for the next year and a half, which was miserable for everyone involved. I then went to high school for three years at a very small, private religious school. I never felt right at that school. I just didn't fit in; my social skills were lacking and I had developed insecurities. I just didn't feel right about myself. There was some unidentified thing wrong with me and I had no idea what it was, but I felt separated from everyone.

My academic grades were very good, and I was actually one year ahead of the other kids my age. By the time I was a junior in high school, I was just fifteen. Halfway through that year a young lady, two years older than me, transferred into my school. She was exactly what I was looking for—she had pink hair with a "V" shaved into the back of her head. I knew she needed help and I appointed myself to do the job. She had had a tough life and had been bounced from one family member to another and eventually wound up at my school.

We spent the next two years together and I was intimately introduced to active alcoholism. She drank every chance she could get and would take any substance that would change her. I became her caregiver, and I loved it. My life finally had meaning; I had a real purpose—to take care of her.

At the age of seventeen I decided it was time for me to move out of my parents' house and get out on my own. I found three other kids (aged sixteen, seventeen, and eighteen) who were looking to do the same thing. We located a house a lady agreed to rent to us—to this day I question her sanity regarding that decision. Perhaps she was drunk at the time.

So, we moved into a very nice house—at least it was nice for the first few weeks. This was my first opportunity to select who I would be living with. Two of the three guys I chose were well on their way to alcoholism, and also used all sorts of other drugs for recreational purposes. The third guy was seemingly normal. He wasn't like them or me—he actually was very well adjusted.

After about a month, the "normal one" had had enough and decided to move back in with his parents. Of course, I responded with anger and resentment, "How can you do this to me and leave me as the only responsible one with these guys?" I began developing a pattern of self-righteous indignation, which lasted for years. My motto could easily have been: "Why am I always the one . . . who has to patch the holes in the walls? . . . talk to the police when they come? . . . pay the bills? . . . clean up after everyone?" And on and on . . .

Never once did I look at the fact that I chose to be there and I chose to stay. Living that way with those guys gave my life a purpose; my job was to take care of everyone, and to do everything. I knew I had to do it regardless of what it was, because if I didn't do it myself it wouldn't be done, or at least it wouldn't be done right. Of course, I was a martyr filled with self-righteousness and contempt for those roommates and all I had to do.

Well, we had to find another roommate to take the place of the one who left. This time we selected one who fit right in. He was also likely an alcoholic, but he had plenty of money since he was a drug dealer. So we were confident that he could pay his share of the rent.

Around that same time I became good friends with one of the original roommates. We hung out together, drank, and partied. I did all the same things as the other guys; the only difference was that I wasn't an alcoholic. I could take it or leave it and never had any problem stopping. My friend starting taking some drugs supplied by the new guy and became immediately hooked. He seemed to become a completely different person overnight. I was very concerned and, as his closest friend, sat him down for a talk—my first attempt at tough love. I explained how I cared about him and was very troubled by what he was doing to himself. I told him that he needed to stop or I wouldn't be able to be his friend anymore. He looked at me and said, "Okay, I'll see ya around." I was devastated that he would choose to continue doing drugs without any consideration of me or our friendship.

As I've learned more about the disease of alcoholism, I have gained a better understanding. I now know that his decision wasn't about me, and he really wasn't capable of making a decision. His illness had affected him to the point that he had no choice in the matter whatsoever. His obsession to drink and use drugs was fueled by either a physical allergy or a physical addiction to the chemicals. The power of choice was no longer available to him and he had no desire to fix a problem he didn't even recognize. As far as he was concerned, he was having a good time and I was overreacting and should probably mind my own business.

The girl I had been dating went away to college in Tennessee after our high school graduation. We stayed in contact and were doing our best at a long-distance relationship. She was coming home for a visit and, of course, weeks ahead I had everything planned as to exactly how we would spend our limited time together that weekend. I cleaned up my little house, which I was proud of, and just wanted to make a good impression. As soon as she arrived, one of my roommates greeted her with a hit of something, which she immediately accepted. For the next nine hours, she sat in the corner studying her hands. This was *not* how I had planned our evening together.

I mention this event because again my reaction was, *"How could you do this to me?"* When, in reality, she didn't do anything to me. She was behaving exactly the way she always had; nothing had changed. I had created an unrealistic mental picture that things would be different this time. For some reason, her behavior that evening was the last straw! I was done; I couldn't take any more of this and decided to end the relationship.

After she returned to school, I called her and told her we were done. I wanted nothing more to do with her and I wouldn't accept any of her calls. The truth is that I was afraid of her and that's why I took the cowardly route and called her. She responded exactly how I thought she would: by having her friends call me and leave messages that she was going to hurt herself and I needed to contact her. I don't know how I managed to not succumb to the requests, but somehow I managed. That was the first time I was able to say "no" and really stick to it.

She did try to reach me periodically for several years through friends or family, but I never responded. After I had been in recovery for several years, I learned she had taken her own life. I'm so grateful that by the time I found this out I had already begun to live by the principles of Al-Anon. Otherwise, I'm sure I would have somehow thought I was to blame for this tragedy; again, I would have found a way to make it "all about me." I felt bad about what happened, but I clearly understood that she was a sick person, not a bad person, and it wasn't about me or anything I did.

One thing I found out about myself after our breakup was that I don't do very well when I don't have someone in my life to obsess about. So it wasn't long until I found my next volunteer "hostage." She was seventeen, still in high school, and having problems at home when we met. I was eighteen at the time. We decided to move in together and for the next four and a half years we proceeded to have the unhealthiest relationship a couple could possibly have.

During our time together we did have some fun—like touring the country in a VW van while I unsuccessfully tried to be a hippie. I say unsuccessfully because it's pretty difficult to be a hippie when you're full of self-centered fear and anxiety, and are schedule-oriented and uptight all the time.

The concept of being a hippie was intriguing and I did master the long hair and beard part of it, but that was as far as I got. The idea of ease and comfort that came from not worrying about anything was so attractive to me—I just could never get anywhere close to grasping it.

As our relationship continued, we decided we would get married and move to Boulder, Colorado, to start our life together. Everyone who knew us could see how miserable we were together—except us. I treated her very poorly and we acted as if we hated each other. I stayed in the relationship for the same reasons I had stayed in every other relationship, job, or friendship. It was the idea that it's not going to get any better than this, I don't deserve better than this, and she desperately needs me. My arrogance was so bad that I really thought she couldn't be without me and I so badly depended on being needed for my own well-being. At that time I believed that the worst, most miserable relationship was infinitely better than the terror of being alone.

At my job I had become friends with a woman named Annie, who I deemed to be way out of my league. She was so mature and had it together—I never considered having somebody like her in my life. Annie knew that I was planning on marrying this girl but was also aware of how unhappy I was in the relationship. As I was preparing to leave for Colorado with my fiancée, Annie decided to give me a letter she had written to me. It basically said that if I was really as miserable as I appeared to be, and would consider changing my mind, that she would like to have a relationship with me. I was completely taken aback and couldn't understand why someone like her would want to be with me.

I announced to my fiancée that I was leaving her. Annie was living with my sister at the time and I moved into my sister's house. I figured it looked like I was living with my sister and not with Annie—at least in my mind. I didn't want my ex-fiancée to know that I had immediately moved in with someone else. I should mention that Annie is a few years older than me and had been a sober member of Alcoholics Anonymous for about four years when we started dating.

We attended open AA meetings together and I fell in love with her and with AA. We decided to get married, and things were going along wonderfully. One evening we were out with a couple of friends having dinner at a restaurant-brewery and the waitress set some sample shots of beer on the table. Annie reached over, took one, and had a sip of it. I certainly didn't know much about alcoholism or AA, but I knew the idea was no alcohol.

Thankfully, this didn't set up a compulsion for her to drink more, and for the most part it had no visible effect on her. Several months later, though, while going through the Steps with a new sponsor, she casually mentioned the sip of beer. To her surprise she was told that she needed to change her sobriety date, which infuriated her. All of a sudden she went from someone who enjoyed recovery and was excited about AA to someone who was belligerent and angry. Something like: "If I'm going to change my sobriety date it's not going to be for a sip of beer—I'll go do it right."

She talked with some of her AA friends about the situation and ultimately decided to change her sobriety date and work through her challenges. It took some time, but she didn't pick up another drink, for which we are both very grateful.

This experience affected me totally differently from her. At first, I thought nothing of the sip of beer, but when I saw her reaction to the suggestion of changing her sobriety date, I was floored. What happened to this happy, energetic, and sober girl I was planning on marrying? I got scared, and concerned, that she would drink again. Of course, my self-centeredness had me worrying more about me than her. I began "walking on egg-shells" hoping to not upset anything for fear that my perfect world would be disturbed.

One night while I was talking to one of Annie's AA friends about all this and describing my concerns and fears, she simply asked me if I knew about Al-Anon. I answered, "Of course." What I knew about Al-Anon came from several uninformed members of AA. So my head said, "Oh no, not me." I knew my place wasn't in Al-Anon.

Fortunately, I had what I refer to as a "gift of desperation" and could no longer go on living the way I was living. I had to do something! I attended my first Al-Anon meeting at the Queen City Group in Charlotte early in the summer of 1999. Of course, I still had the long hair and beard; I was twenty-three years old and completely filled with fear. I thought I would be in a room filled with old ladies, waiting for somebody to tell me I was in the wrong place—which would have been enough to get me to leave and not come back. Instead, I was warmly welcomed and told that I *was* in the right place.

Having never attended an Al-Anon meeting, I had some ex-pectations of what was going to take place. I was so far off base that I'm just grateful the pain was bad enough to get me to go. I figured they would go around the room discussing their loved one's drinking and the damage it was causing them and their family. I'd wait for my turn to tell them that my "soon-to-be wife" had taken a sip of beer. Surprisingly, they weren't talking about anyone other than themselves, their insanity, their defects of character, and how they had found a new way of life. They didn't talk about their alcoholic at all—just about what they were doing to learn to live this spiritual program of recovery.

Over the next few meetings, I began to get a much better understanding of the family disease of alcoholism and a clearer idea that alcohol or drinking is but one symptom of the illness. This answered many of my questions about the behaviors I had seen Annie display, even though she wasn't drinking. I began to see the reactions and behaviors I had developed over the years for dealing with the dysfunctional relationships in my own life. The process was slow and in the beginning I sat in the back of the room, but eventually I began to get more and more comfortable. Annie and I did get married and Al-Anon helped me to better understand her recovery.

Simply by attending meetings I started getting a little better; my focus changed from wanting to fix her to working on myself. I kept hearing people talk about "the Program," meaning the Twelve Steps. Things were said to me like "If you really want to get better, you should get a sponsor." The last thing I wanted to do was to find another man and ask him to help me and to take me through the Steps. I thought I was the one who was supposed to do the helping; my arrogance and fear stood in the way of my growth.

There was a guy I frequently saw at meetings and he always talked about "the solution" and I could see that he was happy. I wanted what he had—although I didn't understand what it was. So after a meeting one day I mustered up all the courage I had and asked him to be my sponsor. Tom replied with a couple questions: "Are you willing to do all the things that I do in this program to get what I've got? Are you willing to pass it on the way it's been given to you?" I answered yes to both, even though I didn't understand the questions.

He proceeded to tell me that he was also an alcoholic and a member of AA. I didn't know that, because the groups I had been attending taught that those who were members of other Twelve Step fellowships should maintain their anonymity regarding those outside issues and focus on Al-Anon. Tom explained to me that the only way he knew to sponsor me was how he'd been sponsored, and he was prepared to take me through the Steps.

We began at Step One and discussed powerlessness. I had already come to terms with my personal powerlessness over my wife and whether or not she drank. But he wanted me to go deeper than that; he wanted me to make a list of everything I was powerless over. This was a very helpful exercise for me, even though it is not found in the Al-Anon literature. Next to each of these points he had me write how my life had become unmanageable when I tried to control these things. This turned out to be a critical part of my recovery because it was important for me to see just how powerless I was over everything in my life that wasn't me. I learned that if it wasn't my reaction, my behavior, or my attitude, I was powerless over it!

I was also able to see that my life wasn't unmanageable because I was powerless over those things. I thought my life was unmanageable because I was powerless over alcohol. What I needed to see was the connection between my unwillingness to accept my powerlessness and the unmanageability. My life only became unmanageable when I refused to accept or admit that I was powerless over the people, places, and things in my life.

I really needed to see that because I had lived my entire life with the insane delusion that if I loved someone she couldn't be okay unless she was doing exactly what I thought she should be doing — or not doing what I thought she shouldn't be doing. In other words, I lived my life knowing that if she would just do what I told her to do, she'd be happy and so would I. And, if for some reason she didn't respond by doing whatever I thought best for her to do, it was because I hadn't properly explained myself. My solution to that dilemma was to keep explaining it in different ways until she did what I wanted, so we could both be happy.

This is not just unmanageability; it's insanity. But, nevertheless, that was how I had functioned. I needed to see that my life was only unmanageable because I continued with this behavior. I needed to find a way to be okay with myself regardless of whether the people I loved were okay or not. For me, that was the miracle of this program, because when I first came in that was absolutely impossible. All I could see was that if she would just get her act together or just be the way she was when we first met—then I'd be okay.

Once I could see my insanity, I became ready to believe that a Power greater than myself could restore me to sanity. My sponsor's help was immeasurable during this process because I had developed so many false beliefs resulting from my early experiences with religion.

When I was ready for Step Three, I made the decision to begin to turn my will and my life over to the care of God. I'm very grateful for the concept of *"as we understood Him."* This notion was something completely foreign to me. The beliefs I was taught as a child would have not only forbidden this concept, but would have guaranteed this concept was a straight shot to hell. I don't think I would have ever learned this idea if it hadn't been for Al-Anon. Without those simple words, I wouldn't have a relationship with the God of my understanding; and without that, I would have nothing. This relationship has become the foundation of my recovery and my life.

By using the Third Step, I deal with fear and anxiety when they creep into my life. I realize that in some way, I'm trying to run the show again. I can then analyze the situation and make a decision to turn that person, place, or circumstance over to the care of God—trusting that it's going to work out exactly the way it's supposed to.

It's probably important for me to mention that when Tom took me through the Twelve Steps, we used the Big Book of *Alcoholics Anonymous* as our main source. I know that this book is not Al-Anon conference approved; however, it is an excellent resource and, in my opinion, the most effective basic text for recovery available. It gives clear directions about taking the Steps.

As I continued with the program, I did a "searching and

fearless moral inventory." This gave me the opportunity to look at *my part* in all these past events. It also put my character defects in a new light; and I could see that once I rid myself of these things I'd be free to really enjoy my life. No longer would I have to depend on others conforming to my demands for happiness. I would work toward allowing God to direct my life.

Once I was able to share all this with another man in my Fifth Step, I began to believe and became willing to let God take the things that were blocking me from Him. I did the Sixth and Seventh Steps as directed and prayed the Seventh Step prayer: "My Creator, I am now willing that you should have all of me, good and bad. I pray that you now remove from me every single defect of character which stands in the way of my usefulness to you and my fellows. Grant me strength, as I go out from here, to do your bidding. Amen."

The next day I woke up and realized that my defects hadn't yet been removed. My sponsor helped me to understand that I was to *humbly* ask God to remove these things. This was not a demand I was to place upon God. I must humbly ask Him, and in God's time these things would be removed. I also believed I had to do my part. For example, if I want guilt to be removed, I need to stop doing things that make me feel guilty. If I want self-centered fear to go away, I have to do things that I fear, trusting that the outcome will be okay, and then the fear will be removed.

By doing the Eighth and Ninth Steps—with a great deal of wisdom and guidance from my sponsor—I was beginning to experience a spiritual awakening. I knew the enormous amount of guilt I had been carrying with me would be lifted by making these amends—not by apologizing, but by righting the wrong and not repeating the behavior. That is where I had to be changed and live by the principles I learned through working the Steps. This process was amazing and my resentments left me. That is when I truly became free.

When taking my Tenth Step, I not only look at those areas where I need to promptly admit something I may have done wrong but also look at the items in stock that are good. I can see that I'm treating people better and becoming more like the person I want to be. I'm able to see that the shelves are filled with good stuff—not the damaged items that I've already dealt with. This is when I acknowledge to myself and to God what the Al-Anon program is doing for me, which also keeps me from slipping back into some morbid reflection or self-pity.

The Eleventh Step is where I focus on letting go of my will and ask God for knowledge of His will for me. Before I came into Al-Anon, the extent of my prayers were of me bargaining with God for something I wanted. Today I am able to try to seek guidance through my prayer and meditation so that I may try to better serve others.

The Twelfth Step reminds me of the spiritual awakening I've been given as a result of taking these Steps. The Step asks me to practice these principles in all that I do. It also asks me to carry this message to others, which is what I do. And each time I go out and give freely in service to others, I benefit. Whether I'm making coffee or setting up chairs, sponsoring somebody or greeting a newcomer, when I get out of myself and serve someone else, I feel good.

I have been taught to surrender myself to the spiritual discipline of the Twelve Steps and to live one day at a time, accepting the grace of God. My life has been transformed. Today I have a great life with my wife, Annie. I work at a job I enjoy, sponsor men in the program, and remain very active in my home group. I have friends in recovery all over the country and get to participate in roundups and conferences in many different states. This is not the life I envisioned when I first entered the rooms of Al-Anon—I never knew it could be this good. ⤙

TWELVE

"Restore Us to Sanity?
I Needed to Be Introduced to Sanity"

Like the story told in chapter 11, this one recounts an Al-Anon member's own experience with the fellowship. Again, this story reflects only the opinions of the person telling it; it does not speak for Al-Anon Family Groups as a whole. The speaker is a woman named Vannoy.[1]

. . . .

There's an AA member in Dallas who told me he once attended a discussion meeting with the topic of "What do you think makes up the disease of alcoholism?" He said they went around the room and each person shared his or her views on what many people refer to as the "isms" of alcoholism. But the really profound thing about this meeting was that not one person mentioned "alcohol."

When I look at my own experience and the experiences of

the many people I have come to know through Al-Anon over the past forty-two years, I can completely relate to this discussion. I suppose if one surveyed Al-Anon's members about the characteristics of what makes up an "Al-Anon," many things would come up, including *"addicted to excitement."* It's likely you wouldn't hear about alcohol either. The key manifestation of our illness is the obsession we have for the alcoholic. At least that was how it was in my particular case.

I grew up in Lubbock, Texas, in a family that consisted of my father, a part Indian from Oklahoma, my mother, who was from a divorced family long before that was fashionable, my three brothers, and me. My daddy owned and ran a successful used furniture business that afforded our family the opportunity to take an occasional vacation. On one such trip to Oklahoma my oldest brother broke his neck and became paralyzed; this event changed our lives forever and deeply affected me. Every resource my parents had went into the care of my brother, which caused a great financial burden for them.

I remember that the front page of our local newspaper showed a picture of my brother in his hospital bed with my dad standing at the foot of the bed. The caption read "Father Swallows Pride and Asks for Help." We began receiving donations from all over the community and lots of visitors came by (most of them from the church) to offer support.

This charity caused me to have many misconceptions about the church and religious people in general. I vividly recall how my parents responded toward this generosity. I can still picture my mother with her head down while tears rolled down her cheeks and Daddy retreating to the backyard with a gray face. Meanwhile, I was being smothered by people telling me that Jesus loved me. I internalized that this was not a good thing; I thought those people were the cause of the tears and I didn't want any part of it.

Sometime later a group of people came over and placed my brother on his mattress in the middle of the floor. They all gathered around and began praying and yelling, screaming and carrying on with some type of healing ritual. It was all very frightening to me as a little kid.

After they left I went in to check on my big brother to see if he was all right. He looked at me and said, "They just did a prayer thing for me and I'm gonna be healed. The first thing I'm going to do is chase you around the backyard."

This thrilled me to death and I went out to the living room and sat on the couch in anticipation of running around the yard with my brother. Of course, it never happened and this became a turning point in my life. I decided those people were wrong and so was the whole idea of God. I determined right then that this "religious stuff" doesn't work and it's not for my life.

After that our house was not a fun place and I pretty much kept to myself. Because of my brother's condition, the house had a constant unpleasant odor and I was embarrassed and filled with shame. Everything was very confusing for me. Between re-ceiving the charity and my own lack of maturity regarding all that was taking place, I began shutting down and became very quiet. I started spending as little time as possible at home and hung out on the streets.

Barely a teenager, I started running with the older kids. I just wanted to escape into a fantasy or dream world. I would see a magazine or a movie and think, "I want this to be my world." Of course, life was always perfect in the movies back then.

When I got a little older, one of my friends who was seven-teen or eighteen, a couple of years my senior, offered to take me to my first honky-tonk. I had heard of those places and I was a little fearful, not knowing what to expect. This became a de-fining moment in my life; I walked in and suddenly everything seemed all right. I can relate this experience to the alcoholic describing taking his first drink—a sense of ease and comfort came over me at once.

It was about eleven o'clock and all the guys were lined up on the side nearest the bar while the girls were lined up on the opposite side of the room. Once a guy had enough to drink he would swagger across the room to one of the girls and ask for a dance. One of my AA friends from Texas said to me, "If you lined up ten pretty girls against the wall, he would pick the sickest one." He obviously hadn't figured out that the sickest one of the ten actually takes one step forward creating the illusion that she's in a class by herself. In my own case, after studying the bar, I would be the one stepping forward.

Now that I had found ease and comfort in these honky-tonks, my dreams and fantasies came along with me. I was going to get married, have two children and a station wagon with wood trim on the side. Rock Hudson always bought one for his wife. And Doris Day was the beautiful wife with everything just perfect. Even the dog was fluffy white. I would see the movies and then escape into my dreams in the clubs at night.

During that time of my life, I began to trade my morals and respectability for my "fix," which happened to be the "alcoholic man." Not just any man would do; my self-worth was reduced to the point that the only men I was able to be around were those who were at least as sick as me. I manipulated them and attempted to mold them into whatever my fantasy happened to be at the time. All dignity had vanished, as did hope for a decent life. When I got a drink for a guy, instead of it being one ounce of whiskey and five ounces of water, I'd do the opposite, knowing that once he was drunk he'd become an easy target for me.

The path I was on led me to know that I had become nothing more than garbage; I was uneducated and clearly a disappointment. The honky-tonks were the only places I knew of to find companionship and, as I mentioned, these were very sick, short relationships. Naturally this is where I met my first major alcoholic. He was a professional gambler and a bootlegger and, as I later learned, a hit man. He was associated with some very shady, underground people in the business of trafficking stolen goods.

The Gambler and I had a little place out in the country which was frequented by his friends and associates. One of my first warnings of the life I had ventured into happened when we arrived home one night. The couple who was staying with us had had a fight earlier in the evening. The man had taken out his pistol and started shooting. He eventually caught the woman and pistol-whipped her, leaving blood all over the walls and doors inside the house.

Needless to say, I was nervous, so to comfort me the Gambler said, "Relax, he's just drunk." And he went into their room and took the gun. He then proceeded to go to bed.

I sat up the entire night wondering, "What in the world am I doing here? How did I get into this? What has happened to me?" All night I contemplated these thoughts.

I decided I had to get away and leave. Just days later I discovered I was pregnant, which left me only one choice: to move back in with him. My parents wanted nothing to do with me. I knew I was nothing more than a disappointment to them and a disgrace to the entire family.

After the baby was born, the Gambler said to me, "Well, I've done all I can for you. Now it's time for you to leave." I took my baby girl and left to stay with a friend.

It wasn't until years later that I recognized how vindictive I had become. My rationalization at the time was, "You hurt me, so let me do something to hurt you so you will see how much pain I'm in." My plan was to go over to the other side of town and pick up a guy I knew the Gambler hated, but I knew liked me. This guy was also an alcoholic I could easily manipulate, which I did. I got him to take me to an after-hours club called the Bloody Bucket so I could show him off in front of the Gambler, who I knew would be there. I hoped to make him jealous so he could see how much he hurt me and just what he was losing.

A couple of days later my friend Juanita knocked at the door and told me that the Gambler had taken a shotgun and blown the guy's head off. I had never expected it and just couldn't believe this was happening. I began to feel pressure in my chest and darkness all around. The pain was engulfing me and was so intense I just couldn't bear it. Right then I made a decision, "I shall not feel this!" I completely blocked it out and moved into denial—stuffing my feelings so deep down inside that it took many years, and doing the Steps with my Al-Anon sponsor, for me to be willing to look at my part in this.

This incident was big news and was splashed all over the papers. Everyone knew I was somehow involved with the Gambler. I went to my parents hoping to find some comfort. Instead, my mother told me that she wanted nothing more to do with me and that if anyone asked me if I was her daughter, to please just say no.

My mother dedicated all of her time taking care of my brother. Her only outlet was her membership in a civic group, where she held a position of state office. As a result of my behavior, my mother was asked to step down from her position, which was, of course, a crushing blow. I held no bad feelings toward my parents because I couldn't blame them and I understood how badly I had disgraced them.

With the walls closing in on me and a constant feeling that something bad was about to happen, I knew I needed to change my lifestyle. My mind went back to those dreams of a good life with a good man. I knew that if I could find the right guy, this time things would be different. Living in Texas, I didn't have many choices for finding a man; it was either a honky-tonk or the rodeo. Since I hadn't done so well with the honky-tonk, I thought I would try the rodeo.

So I headed to the rodeo grounds to find a cowboy who would "fix" me. Now the rodeo grounds are quite a bit different from the honky-tonks. Next to the rodeo was a large slab of concrete with a fence around it. Off to one side was a bar where the cowboys would line up. Across the way, up against the fence, is where the cowgirls lined up. I knew how to pick 'em and it wasn't long before I was all over the dance floor with my bull-rider and, of course, he liked to drink.

We hit it off and continued to see each other, and one evening we were at a honky-tonk. He'd been drinking heavily and proceeded to start poking me in the chest. I decided to grab an almost-empty bottle of beer and whack him over the head with it as hard as I could. This dropped him to his knees and I thought it would be a good time to leave. He chased me out to the car and grabbed me. Spinning me around, he looked me in the eyes and said, "I think you just knocked some sense into me—I think we should get married."

As I said, he was a drinker and liked to have a gallon jug of "salty dog." I kept it filled for him until we were married a few days later. I made sure he didn't draw a sober breath, for fear he would change his mind. I knew that good girls got married and I somehow fantasized that if I were married all my problems would be over and we would start living my dreams. This worked out great for about a week until he bumped into one of his buddies and instead of coming home he went drinking at the local club.

As his drinking continued, my insanity increased and I found myself pacing the floors at night or waiting by the front window until I saw car lights. Then I'd rush to bed so he wouldn't know I was up waiting. Sometimes, my fear and loneliness were so intense I would go out looking for him. Of course, when I did find him there was always a scene, with me acting hysterical, throwing chairs or dragging some unsuspecting girl off the dance floor for a fight. The violence at home often left me bruised with an occasional black eye.

Looking back, I can see that I was using "my man" as my Higher Power. I had literally turned my life and my will over to him. All my thoughts were focused on him, always wanting to fix him so we could resume living the unattainable illusion of the perfect family I had created in my mind. I guess when you have no self-worth, and you feel like garbage, with nobody to look up to and certainly no heroes in your life, you just let yourself get beat up. I was always hoping that somehow, someway, it would all be different tomorrow. The feelings of guilt I carried with me all the time allowed me to accept the beatings as if I somehow deserved them. I'm not sure why I felt guilty all the time—I just did!

My sickness dictated my actions and I knew that somehow I needed to make this work out. My madness kept me in fear and my dreams were slipping away. I knew if this marriage failed I would just disintegrate and fall into some imaginary hole and never come out. Perhaps this obsession to control and to make things turn out right is on some level similar to the alcoholic's desire to control and enjoy their drinking. The book *Alcoholics Anonymous* states, "Therefore, it is not surprising that our drinking careers have been characterized by countless vain attempts to prove we could drink like other people."[2]

I became pregnant, thinking this would solve the problem. If he only had a son, he would change and things would be better. But it wasn't long before he was taking our little boy off to the rodeo, putting him on a bull, and letting him ride. I'd be frantic in the grandstand, causing a scene, screaming, "GET OFF THE BULL!"

Alcoholism took over our lives and I got sicker and sicker. My behavior was hideous and I just couldn't stop nagging, controlling, and fighting. The disease wasn't just progressive for the alcoholic; it was progressing within me—building a condition of hopelessness in my life. I didn't want to be the way I was; I just didn't know any other way to be.

I wasn't proud of what I had become. My two children feared me more than they did my alcoholic husband. They witnessed insanity and rage that is indescribable. No innocent child should ever have to see it, let alone live with it. My father came by every once in a while because he absolutely adored my children, and perhaps he was the only stable person those two kids knew.

The darkness grew for me and I lost all hope. I found myself sitting alone in a rocking chair wishing for the courage to commit suicide. I only wanted to die for a little while, just long enough to stop the pain. Sitting there one morning, I remembered reading an Ann Landers article in the newspaper about the wife of an alcoholic. It was suggested that she call Alcoholics Anonymous.

I got up from the chair, looked up the AA number, and made the call. The conversation resulted in an invitation to the house of a woman who was a sober member of Alcoholics Anonymous. When I arrived, she walked me through the living room and kitchen to the den in the back of the house. It's funny how well I remember that day, and one thing that really caught my eye was her kitchen. It was sparkling clean; the white sink was just as shiny as can be and the long table had a tablecloth on it and it looked beautiful. I was wondering where all the dishes were, because the sink was empty. In my house, if you needed a dish, you went to the sink and washed one—I didn't have time to wash dishes.

She and I sat and talked for quite awhile and were joined by her husband when he arrived home. He was also a sober member of AA. I don't know why God chose this particular route for me, but I'm forever grateful. As those people were talking to me that day, something began to happen to me. A little spark of hope was lit as I sat with those two members of Alcoholics Anonymous.

The couple arranged to pick me up to take me to my first meeting later that night. When we got there, the husband held the door for me. I was confused, because I wasn't sure why he was doing it; nobody held doors for me. That was a privilege reserved for "ladies" and I certainly didn't see myself as a lady. I'm not sure exactly what happened to me right then, but it was as if music began to play.

As I entered the clubhouse, I saw two alcoholics at the other end of the room standing close to the cigarette machine. The machine was illuminated and the light reflected off these two men, and I noticed they were both laughing. I had not heard or seen laughter in a very long time. There is no laughter in an alcoholic home, at least not mine.

The Al-Anon meeting was in the other room. and I sat there and just listened. I don't know what they said; I was so self-absorbed and in so much pain it just didn't matter what they said. But I knew I was safe! It's funny, sometimes I hear someone make a comment about what's said in a meeting, such as "If anyone had done or said that when I was new, I would have left." I had nowhere to go, and for that matter, it wasn't so much what I heard that got me—it was what I felt! And that's what got me to come back.

As I kept coming back, I began to make some friends. Somebody gave me a book, *The Prophet* by Kahlil Gibran. There's a line in the book that has meant so much to me: "When you love you should not say, 'God is in my heart,' but rather, 'I am in the heart of God.'"[3] That is what I felt when I began going to meetings. There is a spirit present in every meeting that I've ever been to. Sometimes I'm too tired or distracted to feel it, but I know it's there.

By attending meetings I began to hear what was being said and suggested. I heard about sponsorship and the Steps; I could see the Steps hanging on the wall. I also heard about God. At first I wanted to be there but didn't feel comfortable with people. So I would slip in just as the meeting started and slip out as soon as it closed so I could avoid any real contact.

One night as I was trying to slip out, "she caught me." A little lady named Pat started telling me about herself and she just made me feel welcome. I immediately knew I could trust her. Looking back on that night, I see this was one of God's divine appointments.

A few days later I told someone that Pat was my sponsor, although I hadn't asked her. The very next day she showed up at the drugstore where I was working. We talked for a short while. When she was leaving, she extended her hand and said, "I want to thank you for trusting me," as she slipped a ten-dollar bill into my hand. This was in February of 1969 and ten dollars was

a lot of money for me. Her timing couldn't have been more perfect because the electricity was about to be shut off, I had no
food for the two kids, and the gas tank was on empty.

Sometime later, Pat taught me a very important lesson about
giving when I tried to give the ten dollars back to her. She said,
"No, you're to pass it on to somebody else who needs it worse
than you." She explained that this is what we do, and by giving
what I have I open myself up to receive more. I can tell you that
same ten dollars has multiplied many times over the years and
has helped countless others in need.

Pat also bought the Big Book of *Alcoholics Anonymous* for
me. She told me that we study it to learn about the disease of
alcoholism so we know what we're dealing with. She couldn't
know then that I'd eventually have a child and a grandchild in-
flicted with this horrible disease.

Pat told me that after I had read the book we would go back
through it and begin working the Steps. So she took me through
the Steps of the program. We also read and studied other books
including one of my favorites, *One Day at a Time in Al-Anon,*
which had just recently been published by Al-Anon Family
Group Headquarters. July 1st is my favorite entry in the book,
and I've recommended the book to everyone.

I met with my sponsor on a regular basis and attended a lot
of meetings. Progress was slow in the beginning, perhaps because of my lack of belief in God. I heard people talk about God
but I couldn't identify. My personal experience was confined to
the contact I had with the church folks when they came to heal
my oldest brother when he broke his neck. I saw no evidence of
any God and just dismissed Him out of my mind. I wasn't confused or caught in some type of denial necessarily; I simply saw
nothing to convince me of anything different.

About six months after I started going to Al-Anon, I was sitting in a meeting and was absently looking at the Steps hanging on the wall. I suddenly really noticed the second part of the

Third Step, and it struck me: "God *as we understood Him.*" That was it! I could start right there. That is when I finally became willing to follow the directions of the program.

I met with Pat shortly after that experience and shared with her what had happened. She reached over, pulled out the AA Big Book, turned to page 46, and read the following: "God does not make too hard terms with those who seek Him. To us, the Realm of Spirit is broad, roomy, all inclusive; never exclusive or forbidding to those who earnestly seek. It is open, we believe, to all men."[4] She then said, "Think of yourself being in the basement of a house and God is on the rooftop. He's not waiting for you to come up to meet Him. He'll come down and meet you right where you are."

As we went through the Steps, I wrote out each one and how it applied to me at the time. For the First Step, I looked at all of the areas in my life where I was powerless; I was powerless over the "cowboy," I was powerless over "my children," and so on. Then I proceeded to Step Two the same way. When I was doing this Step, it was suggested that I look back at all the major events in my life to see if I could see the hand of God. It started becoming very clear that God was with me all along; I just wasn't aware of His presence.

Then I took my Third Step on my knees and it was as if I was being wrapped in a warm blanket of spirit. I knew fully then that there was a God and I've been working on my relationship with Him ever since.

Things at home weren't really getting better, but I was. He was gone most of the time, but after a while he started catching on that something in me was changing. When he figured out what it was, he tried to stop me from going to meetings. After about a year he decided to go to AA and he got sober for about six months. He attended one of the conventions and heard some wonderful speakers, but afterwards he decided that he wasn't an alcoholic.

I stayed with him for seven years after I began my journey

forward with Al-Anon. It took me that long to get sufficient sanity to see that I really did need to leave him. I have a friend in AA who said, "We're not restored to sanity—we're introduced to it." That certainly applied to me.

Once I started attending meetings, the physical violence at home stopped—perhaps because one of my alcoholic friends suggested that I keep my mouth shut. However, after seven years he came home one particular night with a wild glaze in his eyes and I suspected he was in a blackout. I could tell he was in a rage when he began to beat me up. I became tangled in the sheets and fell off the bed onto the floor face first. It was as if I bounced when I hit the floor and, when I did, I could see my two children standing in the doorway screaming, tears rolling down their cheeks as they begged him to stop. Seeing their faces gave me the courage to get out of there, and I filed for divorce.

One of the reasons I stayed with him so long was what I call the "soon as" syndrome. Whenever somebody said, "Why don't you leave him? It's a choice, you know." I'd say verbally or silently, "I am leaving him; just as soon as the car gets paid off, or I get some money saved, or when the kids get out of school." The truth is, I had no more idea of why I stayed with him than the alcoholic has of why he takes the first drink. I guess I, like the alcoholic, needed to hit bottom.

After leaving him, I knew I needed some kind of a career. I had no real education because I had dropped out of high school. I decided to attend nursing school, and at graduation the entire front section was filled with my AA and Al-Anon friends and family. I was given the privilege of delivering the class response to the invited guests. As I was making my speech, I looked out over the crowd and could see my parents sitting there. Daddy was kicking the chair of his neighbor. Mr. Stewart leaned forward and Daddy said, "That's my daughter up there."

There have been so many occasions in my life when I am overwhelmed with gratitude for the new life that has been given to me. I've had many opportunities to make amends and learn

how to live by the Twelve Steps. I haven't done any of this perfectly, and some things have taken many years to change. That
is why they told me we do this one day at a time. I wish I never
made any mistakes, but the truth is I have. I don't have regrets
today, and in many ways my life is a dream come true.

In 1980, I met Jim, a sober member of Alcoholics Anonymous,
at a convention. We became friends and started a long-distance
relationship that lasted about nine months before we decided
that I should move out to California to be close to him. The plan
was that I would get an apartment and find a job. We would
continue dating and eventually get married. It was important
to both of us that we do this the "right way." But before I could
move, Jim flew down to Lubbock and told me he had changed
his mind and couldn't do it, so we stopped seeing each other.

About two years later, he decided to move back to Oklahoma
where he had lived twenty-five years earlier. He attended the
Midland, Texas, AA conference, hoping to see me, and I was
there. Incidentally, it was the same conference where we had
originally met. We started dating again and married six months
later, in May of 1982. We had some wonderful times together. He
had two children also and we really have a great family.

We moved to LA, then later to Palm Springs, and life was
wonderful. Business appeared to be good and we were looking
forward to a great life. One day Jim came home complaining of
pain in his shoulder. It turned out to be cancer and he died just
three months later. Around that same time, it was discovered
that the business manager had been embezzling money. When
Jim died, I was left with nothing.

I moved back to LA and had to start over, securing a full-
time job and sharing an apartment until I could get one on my
own. Over the next ten years, I kept busy working and staying
very active in Al-Anon. I have pretty consistently attended two
to three Al-Anon meetings and one open AA meeting every
week since I first began in February of 1969. In 2006, the company I was working for downsized and I lost my job. I have since

moved back to Texas, where I'm very happy and continue to be involved in the program.

The programs of AA and Al-Anon have deeply affected each one of our children and grandchildren, although in different ways. I have been blessed to remain close to all of them and am truly grateful for all we share together.

Some of the things that have become a foundation for my life include my attendance at meetings, sponsorship (both having one and being one), and working and reworking the Twelve Steps. Pat was my sponsor for my first forty years in the program until she died and I had to find another sponsor.

One of the greatest things I've witnessed in my life is the love between two sober alcoholics. It's like nothing else on earth. While I was living in Los Angeles, I attended the Wednesday night open AA meeting of the Pacific Group. This group regularly has one thousand or more people in attendance. I can't tell you how many times I've seen a brand-new alcoholic invited to the podium to read a section of chapter five, "How It Works," from the book *Alcoholics Anonymous*. As he stands there, barely able to speak and obviously not a very good reader, you can see all the alcoholics in the room leaning forward as if to help pull the words out of the new man as he struggles to finish. When he finally completes his task with fear and embarrassment and relief that it's over, the entire audience erupts with approval, much to the newcomer's astonishment. These little things can become life-changing experiences and are common practice among the alcoholics. I'm grateful for each and every one of them.

Having lived in Texas for the majority of my forty-two years in the Al-Anon Family Group fellowship, I have been acquainted with some absolutely wonderful people and some of Al-Anon's pioneers. I knew Arbutus very well, along with Marcy W. and her husband, Bob, and Jack and Pat C. These people touched me deeply, and the AA's and Al-Anon's were one big family. Today, unfortunately, it seems our two fellowships are getting more and more separated. I pray that the rigidity looming over the

Family Groups will lift, and we can focus again on "our common welfare," recognizing that our personal progress as well as the progress of the fellowship depends upon "unity."

I believe that would happen if each Al-Anon member and each group would study and attempt to live by our Traditions, especially the Fifth Tradition, which states: "Each Al-Anon Family Group has but one purpose: to help families of alcoholics. We do this by practicing the Twelve Steps of AA *ourselves*, by encouraging and understanding our alcoholic relatives, and by welcoming and giving comfort to families of alcoholics." This simple formula seems to me to be the answer to many current issues we are facing as individuals and as a society.

The book *One Day at a Time in Al-Anon* has a page that has been so meaningful to me through the years: "This I learned in Al-Anon, says a member at a meeting, that the man I married cannot be the source of my happiness or sorrow. The gift of life is personally mine—as his life belongs to him—to enjoy or destroy, as each of us wishes."[5] I tell my friends to change the phrase "the man I married" and replace it with the name of "their alcoholic," be it a child, a parent, or whoever.

My friend from Texas, Bob W., always gave wonderful AA talks. One day he spoke about how we close our meetings with the Lord's Prayer; then he broke the prayer down and discussed each part. He paused when he got to the final phrase, "for Thine is the kingdom, and the power and the glory, forever." He then said, "If there's a kingdom, there must be a king; if He's our Father, then we must be children of a king, therefore making us royalty. This makes you and me a prince or a princess—so claim your heritage." He challenged us to be who God intended us to be—children of God. And thanks to Al-Anon Family Groups, I truly know I am a child of God. ⌒

EPILOGUE

Celebrating Sixty Years of Al-Anon Family Groups

A CLOSE FRIEND of mine often says, "If we look back through the circumstances and events that have led us to where we are today, we will see how God has pulled a golden thread through each one of them." As I completed this book about the events and circumstances that led to the founding and growth of the Al-Anon Family Group movement, I was in complete agreement with his statement.

I can imagine the excitement and surprise of Lois W. and Anne B. when fifty groups responded to their first mailing in 1951. It's doubtful, however, that they ever envisioned the 25,000 Al-Anon groups that exist today.

So what has changed in sixty years? Alcoholism is still wreaking havoc and destruction within many homes in this country and throughout the world. Children are growing up in abusive homes, learning fear instead of love while seeing firsthand the devastation and horrors of alcoholism. Mothers and fathers are still spending sleepless nights worrying about the teenager who hasn't come home for days and wondering when the phone will ring. And families are scraping the money together to pay for the unexpected funeral of a loved one who just couldn't be helped.

Yes, unfortunately, in many ways things seem worse today than they were sixty years ago. Perhaps in the 1950s when Al-Anon first started we lived in simpler times. Today, watching television or going onto the Internet, we can quickly see the effects and hopelessness facing many families because of alcoholism and other addictions.

We see celebrities and sports heroes making headlines related to alcohol abuse, and we can even follow their successes and failures instantly on Facebook, Twitter, and other Internet sources. Treatment facilities have long waiting lists, and courts are mandating the sick to attend Twelve Step programs. There are hit television reality shows that focus on intervention treatment, and in the popular press we hear recovery language known only to people in Twelve Step programs sixty years ago.

The damage that alcoholism does to the family continues as it has always done. Bill W., when writing the Big Book, said, "The alcoholic is like a tornado roaring his way through the lives of others."[1]

Fortunately, the pioneering members of Al-Anon recognized that they needed a program to help themselves get well. They came to recognize alcoholism as a family illness, and they gained the knowledge that whether or not the alcoholic recovered was secondary. Al-Anon Family Groups help the individual family member or friend to recover from his or her own sickness. For sixty years, despairing wives, parents, children, and friends have found a safe harbor within the rooms of Al-Anon.

Hope has been restored to the hopeless, and countless millions of lives have been changed because of the spiritual tools used within the Al-Anon fellowship. Bill W. often talked about emotional sobriety—Al-Anon members know a thing or two about that—for isn't that likely the goal of each new member when he or she first walks over the threshold of Al-Anon? Many of these people came in feeling as if they carried the weight of a thousand lifetimes, but found peace and serenity beyond their comprehension once they connected with the Al-Anon fellowship.

Having been very close to many Al-Anon members over the years, I understand how truly thankful they are for recovery in their own lives. As Al-Anon members move into the next decade and face the challenges that lie ahead, they can be proud of the successes of the past sixty years. Indeed, they can look forward to the fellowship continuing to grow and serve those who want it. I've heard it said that "It's not for those who need it—it's for those who want it." That simple attitude seems to be paramount in the process of recovery.

Each year Al-Anon Family Groups face not only the changes families are going through within our culture but the changes within their own groups. Not unlike other Twelve Step programs struggling to "carry the message," Al-Anon will need its groups and the individual members to continue to uphold the Twelve Traditions.

Poet and philosopher George Santayana famously said, "Those who cannot remember the past are condemned to repeat it." Al-Anon members have learned this in their homes and groups. By practicing the principles of the Twelve Steps and Twelve Traditions, Al-Anon Family Groups will surely be here helping the next generation and all those to come, for however long it is needed.

With heartfelt appreciation I say thank you, Al-Anon, for sixty years of dedicated service to the alcoholic family. I believe that the pioneering members would be grateful to you for a job well done.

May God bless you and keep you, and happy anniversary!

APPENDIX A

Anne S.

ANNE S. has taken her leave of us. She died on Wednesday June 1. To the hundreds who really knew her, this was a meaningful and moving event. With those who knew her not, I wish to share the inspiration which she gave to Lois and me. Anne was the wife of Dr. Bob, co-founder of Alcoholics Anonymous. She was, quite literally, the mother of our first Group, Akron No. One.

Her wise and beautiful counsel to all, her insistence that the spiritual come before anything else, her unwavering support of Dr. Bob in all his works—all these were virtues which watered the uncertain seed that was to become A.A. Who but God could assess such a contribution? We can only say that it was priceless and magnificent. In the full sense of the word, she was one of the founders of Alcoholics Anonymous.

Not a soul who knew Anne will say that she is really gone. Each knows that her abiding love and influence will live forever. And none knows better than Dr. Bob, Lois and I, who saw these things from the beginning. Nor do we think we shall never see her again. For, like nearly all our fellow A.A. members, we believe there is no death. She is only out of our sight and hearing for a little while.

—*Bill W.*

AA Grapevine, *July 1949*

APPENDIX B

Al-Anon's Twelve Steps

1. We admitted we were powerless over alcohol—that our lives had become unmanageable.
2. Came to believe that a Power greater than ourselves could restore us to sanity.
3. Made a decision to turn our will and our lives over to the care of God *as we understood Him.*
4. Made a searching and fearless moral inventory of ourselves.
5. Admitted to God, to ourselves, and to another human being the exact nature of our wrongs.
6. Were entirely ready to have God remove all these defects of character.
7. Humbly asked Him to remove our shortcomings.
8. Made a list of all persons we had harmed, and became willing to make amends to them all.
9. Made direct amends to such people wherever possible, except when to do so would injure them or others.
10. Continued to take personal inventory and when we were wrong promptly admitted it.
11. Sought through prayer and meditation to improve our conscious contact with God *as we understood Him,* praying only for knowledge of His will for us and the power to carry that out.
12. Having had a spiritual awakening as the result of these steps, we tried to carry this message to others, and to practice these principles in all our affairs.

APPENDIX C

Al-Anon's Twelve Traditions

1. Our common welfare should come first; personal progress for the greatest number depends upon unity.
2. For our group purpose there is but one authority—a loving God as He may express Himself in our group conscience. Our leaders are but trusted servants—they do not govern.
3. The relatives of alcoholics, when gathered together for mutual aid, may call themselves an Al-Anon Family Group, provided that, as a group, they have no other affiliation. The only requirement for membership is that there be a problem of alcoholism in a relative or friend.
4. Each group should be autonomous, except in matters affecting another group or Al-Anon or AA as a whole.
5. Each Al-Anon Family Group has but one purpose: to help families of alcoholics. We do this by practicing the Twelve Steps of AA *ourselves*, by encouraging and understanding our alcoholic relatives, and by welcoming and giving comfort to families of alcoholics.
6. Our Family Groups ought never endorse, finance or lend our name to any outside enterprise, lest problems of money, property and prestige divert us from our primary spiritual aim. Although a separate entity, we should always co-operate with Alcoholics Anonymous.
7. Every group ought to be fully self-supporting, declining outside contributions.
8. Al-Anon Twelfth Step work should remain forever non-professional, but our service centers may employ special workers.

9. Our groups, as such, ought never be organized; but we may create service boards or committees directly responsible to those they serve.

10. The Al-Anon Family Groups have no opinion on outside issues; hence our name ought never be drawn into public controversy.

11. Our public relations policy is based on attraction rather than promotion; we need always maintain personal anonymity at the level of press, radio, films, and TV. We need guard with special care the anonymity of all AA members.

12. Anonymity is the spiritual foundation of all our Traditions, ever reminding us to place principles above personalities.

Al-Anon's Twelve Concepts of Service

1. The ultimate responsibility and authority for Al-Anon world services belongs to the Al-Anon groups.
2. The Al-Anon Family Groups have delegated complete administrative and operational authority to their Conference and its service arms.
3. The right of decision makes effective leadership possible.
4. Participation is the key to harmony.
5. The rights of appeal and petition protect minorities and insure that they be heard.
6. The Conference acknowledges the primary administrative responsibility of the Trustees.
7. The Trustees have legal rights while the rights of the Conference are traditional.
8. The Board of Trustees delegates full authority for routine management of Al-Anon Headquarters to its executive committees.
9. Good personal leadership at all service levels is a necessity. In the field of world service the Board of Trustees assumes the primary leadership.
10. Service responsibility is balanced by carefully defined service authority and double-headed management is avoided.
11. The World Service Office is composed of selected committees, executives and staff members.
12. The spiritual foundation for Al-Anon's world services is contained in the General Warranties of the Conference, Article 12 of the Charter.

Notes

For information on the archival sources cited here, see the author's preface, page xiii.

Preface

1. *Alcoholics Anonymous,* 4th edition (New York: Alcoholics Anonymous World Services, 2001), pp. 58–59.

Chapter One: 855 Ardmore Avenue: The Story of Anne S.

1. Bill W., "Anne S.," *AA Grapevine,* July 1949, p. 6. See appendix A.
2. Bob S., Jr., and Betty S., audio interview by Bill O., April 2, 1975. Midwest Tape Library.
3. Bob S., Jr., audio interview by Don B., December 8, 2001, transcribed by author. Fitzpatrick Archive, www.recoveryspeakers.org.
4. Bill W., interview by Martha Deane, Martha Deane Show, WOR-AM radio program, New York City, May 12, 1956. Record in Recovery Speakers Library.
5. Ibid.
6. Ibid.
7. Bob S., Jr., audio interview by Don B., December 8, 2001.
8. Bob S., Jr., and Betty S., audio interview by Bill O., April 2, 1975.
9. Lois W., speech at Twelfth Southeastern Regional AA Convention, held jointly with Ninth Mississippi State Convention, Biloxi, MS, August 24, 1956, transcribed by author. Fitzpatrick Archive, www.recoveryspeakers .org.
10. Letters originally donated by Bob S., Jr., to Midwest Tape Library (when owned by Bill and Arbutus O.); currently located in Fitzpatrick Archive.

11. Anne S., untitled audio recording made by George H., of Detroit, June 29, 1947, in bedroom of Anne S. at 855 Ardmore Avenue, Akron, OH; then brought to Bill and Lois W. in New York. Now in Fitzpatrick Archive, www.recoveryspeakers.org.

12. Bill W., "Anne S.," *AA Grapevine,* July 1949, p. 6. See appendix A.

13. Bob S., farewell speech, First International Convention of AA, Cleveland, OH, July 30, 1950, transcribed by author. Fitzpatrick Archive, www.recoveryspeakers.org.

14. Lois W., *Lois Remembers: Memoirs of the Co-founder of Al-Anon and Wife of the Co-founder of Alcoholics Anonymous* (New York: Al-Anon Family Group Headquarters, 1979), p. 173. Reprinted with permission.

Chapter Two: The Traveler: Myrtle L.

1. "The Non-alcoholics—God Bless 'Em!" *AA Grapevine,* July 1950, pp. 22–23.

2. Myrtle L., speech given at Twelfth Southeastern Regional AA Convention, held jointly with Ninth Mississippi State Convention, July 24, 1956; and a speech given before a group of AA and Al-Anon members (undated; city unknown) recapping Myrtle's trip to the Ontario Regional AA Conference, March 28, 1953. The tape ended abruptly and Myrtle recorded the remainder of the message later, then sent the entire tape to Bill and Arbutus O. Fitzpatrick Archive.

3. Myrtle L., letter to Arbutus O., Texas Al-Anon members, March 20, 1976. Midwest Tape Library, Fitzpatrick Archive.

Chapter Three: Sound Homes: The First International Convention of AA

1. Lois W., introduction to wives' meeting speakers, First International Convention of AA, Cleveland, OH, July 29, 1950, typed transcription, Fitzpatrick Archive.

2. Pearl E., "Sound Homes through Wives Approach to AA," talk presented to wives' meeting at First International Convention of AA, Cleveland, OH, July 29, 1950, untyped transcription (typed later for archiving), Fitzpatrick Archive.

3. Edith B., "Teamwork in the Home," talk presented to wives' meeting at First International Convention of AA, Cleveland, OH, July 29, 1950, Fitzpatrick Archive.

4. Anne S., "Personal Serenity through Practicing AA Principles in All My Affairs," talk presented to wives' meeting at First International Conven-

tion of AA, Cleveland, OH, July 29, 1950, Fitzpatrick Archive. This version of the Twelfth Step was used by early Family Groups.

5. Anna A., "Harmony and Unity in Our Home," talk presented to wives' meeting at First International Convention of AA, Cleveland, OH, July 29, 1950, Fitzpatrick Archive.

6. Ione G., "Happy Homes through the Miracle of AA," talk presented to wives' meeting at First International Convention of AA, Cleveland, OH, July 29, 1950, Fitzpatrick Archive.

Chapter Four: Experience, Strength, and Hope

These talks were transcribed by Myrtle L. and given to Bill and Arbutus O.

1. Bertha M., "Keys to Better Understanding: Hope," talk given to Family Group panel at Ontario Regional AA Conference, March 26, 1955; written transcription, Fitzpatrick Archive.

2. Helen M., "Keys to Better Understanding: Courage" talk given to Family Group panel at Ontario Regional AA Conference, March 26, 1955; written transcription, Fitzpatrick Archive.

3. Babette B., "Keys to Better Understanding: Growth," talk given to Family Group panel at Ontario Regional AA Conference, March 26, 1955; written transcription, Fitzpatrick Archive.

4. Enid T., "Keys to Better Understanding: Faith," talk given to Family Group panel at Ontario Regional AA Conference, March 26, 1955; written transcription, Fitzpatrick Archive.

Chapter Five: Laying the Foundation for Al-Anon

1. Conversation with author, May 2006.

2. Anonymous, "AA Auxiliary Ritual," handwritten document, undated, Fitzpatrick Archive.

3. Anonymous, "Non-Alcoholics Anonymous Twelve Steps," handwritten document, undated, Fitzpatrick Archive.

4. Non-Alcoholics Anonymous, "Guide to Non-Alcoholics Anonymous of Greater Vancouver," pamphlet, undated, Fitzpatrick Archive.

5. Toronto Family Groups, pamphlet, undated, Fitzpatrick Archive.

6. Ruth G., ed., "How to Live with Alcoholics," *San Francisco Family Forum*, Vol. 4, No., 1, November 1952, p. 9.

7. Lois W., untitled message, *San Francisco Family Forum*, November 1952, p. 7.

8. Margaret D., ed., Editor's Note in *Family Group Forum* (Clearing House), Vol 1. No. 9, September 1954, p. 1.

Chapter Six: "I Knew It Was Time to Tell My Story": Margaret D.

1. Margaret D., untitled speech at Fifth Al-Anon Rally, Detroit, MI, February 23, 1964, audio recording transcribed by author, Fitzpatrick Archive, www.recoveryspeakers.org.

2. Margaret D., speech given April 18, 1978 in New York City; typed copy given to Arbutus O. by Margaret D., Fitzpatrick Archive.

Chapter Seven: Articles from the *AA Grapevine*

Note: Reprinted here with permission, all articles have been retreived from the Grapevine Digital Archives. Some discrepancies exist between the digital and print archives.

1. Lois W., speech given at Texas Convention, Dallas, TX, June 29, 1973, audio recording transcribed by author, Fitzpatrick Archive, www.recoveryspeakers.org.

2. Anonymous, "Points of View," *AA Grapevine*, July 1944, p. 2.

3. Grace O., "Express Your Appreciation," *AA Grapevine*, August 1946, p. 5.

4. Author unknown, "PO Box 1475: An Address Bringing Hope and Help to AA Families," *AA Grapevine*, April 1952, p. 20. Submission by Al-Anon Family Groups.

5. Mrs. C. J. (of Miami), "Encouragement for New Members' Wives in NAA," *AA Grapevine*, March 1952, p. 32.

Chapter Eight: Messages from AA's Cofounder to the Family Groups

1. Bill W., letter to Dr. Abram Hoffer, April 21, 1959, Stepping Stones Archive.

2. Lois W., letter to Bill W., January 24, 1957, Stepping Stones Archive.

3. Bill W., letter to Lois W., January 24, 1957, Stepping Stones Archive.

4. Bill W., speech in Salt Lake City, UT, June 1951, transcribed from audio recording by author, Fitzpatrick Archive, www.recoveryspeakers.org.

5. Margaret D., Al-Anon historical recap, untitled, undated; Stepping Stones Archives.

6. Bill W., speech at Texas State Convention, June 13, 1954, transcribed from audio recording by author, Fitzpatrick Archive, www.recoveryspeakers.org.

7. Arbutus O., conversation with author, May 20, 2006.

8. Ibid.
9. Arbutus O., phone conversation with author, February 2001.
10. Bill W., speech at First Al-Anon World Service Conference, George Washington Hotel, New York City, April 21, 1961, transcript of audio recording, Fitzpatrick Archive.
11. Ibid.
12. Bill W., "World Services," speech at Chelsea School, following Al-Anon World Service Conference, April 1968; transcribed by author, Fitzpatrick Archive; audio at www.recoveryspeakers.org.

Chapter Nine: "We Need This for Ourselves": The Lois W. Story

1. Compiled from two sources: Lois W., talk at Twelfth Southeastern Regional AA Convention, held jointly with Ninth Mississippi State Convention, Biloxi, MS, August 24, 1956; and Lois W., talk at a recovery conference in Topeka, KS, October 17, 1975.
2. Lois W., "Outpouring," undated but written in 1928, Stepping Stones Archives.
3. Lois W., undated letter to Bill from Washington, DC, 1929, Stepping Stones Archives.
4. Bill W., letter to Lois, December 11, 1934, Stepping Stones Archives.
5. Lois W., undated note; apparently written for posterity, ca. late 1970s.
6. Bill W., "Bill's Story," Alcoholics Anonymous, 4th edition (New York: Alcoholics Anonymous World Services, 2001), pp. 13–14.
7. Lois W., talk in Topeka, KS, October 17, 1975.
8. Lois W., letter to Bill, January 24, 1950, Stepping Stones Archives.
9. Lois W., talk in Topeka, KS, October 17, 1975.
10. Ibid.
11. Lois W., letter to National Association for Children of Alcoholics; quotation from Inside Al-Anon, an Al-Anon Family Groups publication, April/May 1986.
12. Ibid.

Chapter Ten: Anne B.'s Story: Co-founder of Al-Anon

1. Author conversation with nephew of Tom P., February 2011.
2. Lois W., speech at DARR conference, a recovery event in Palm Springs, CA, June 4, 1983, audio recording transcribed by author, Fitzpatrick Archive; audio at www.recoveryspeakers.org.

3. Anne B., minutes from Clearing House meeting held at Stepping Stones, November 17, 1951, Stepping Stones Archive.

4. "Family Groups Meet," bulletin from Second AA International Convention, St. Louis, MO, July 1, 1955, Fitzpatrick Archive.

5. Anne B., speech at DARR conference, Palm Springs, CA, June 4, 1983, audio recording transcribed by author, Fitzpatrick Archive; audio at www.recoveryspeakers.org.

6. Ibid. Although Anne B. cites Walt Whitman, the poet here is unverified.

Chapter Eleven: "I Needed a Meeting Long Before I Picked Up My First Drunk"

1. Aaron, February 2011 audio interview with author, and talk at South Carolina Convention by Young People in Alcoholics Anonymous, 2007 (exact date unknown).

Chapter Twelve: "Restore Us to Sanity? I Needed to Be Introduced to Sanity"

1. Vannoy, audio interview with author, January 20, 2011.

2. *Alcoholics Anonymous,* 4th edition (New York: Alcoholics Anonymous World Services, 2001), p. 30.

3. Gibran, Kahlil, *The Prophet* (New York: Knopf, 1971), p. 14.

4. *Alcoholics Anonymous,* p. 46.

5. *One Day at a Time in Al-Anon* (New York: Al-Anon Family Group Headquarters, Inc., 1973), p. 183.

Epilogue: Celebrating Sixty Years of Al-Anon Family Groups

1. *Alcoholics Anonymous,* 4th edition (New York: Alcoholics Anonymous World Services, 2001), p. 82.

Permissions

Quotation on page 20 from *Lois Remembers,* copyright 1979, by Al-Anon Family Group Headquarters, Inc. Reprinted by permission of Al-Anon Family Group Headquarters, Inc. Al-Anon's Twelve Traditions (appendix C) and Twelve Concepts of Service (appendix D) copyright by Al-Anon Family Group Headquarters, Inc. Reprinted by permission of Al-Anon Family Group Headquarters, Inc. Permission to reprint these excerpts does not mean that Al-Anon Family Group Headquarters, Inc. has reviewed or approved the contents of this publication, or that Al-Anon Family Group Headquarters, Inc. necessarily agrees with the views expressed herein. Al-Anon is a program of recovery for families and friends of alcoholics—use of this excerpt in any non Al-Anon context does not imply endorsement or affiliation by Al-Anon.

The Twelve Steps of Alcoholics Anonymous, which also serve as Al-Anon's Twelve Steps (appendix B), are reprinted from *Alcoholics Anonymous,* 4th edition (New York: Alcoholics Anonymous, Inc. 2001).

Chapter 7 includes four articles reprinted from the *AA Grapevine*: page 108, "Points of View," July 1944; page 110, "Express Your Appreciation," August 1946; "PO Box 1475," April 1952; and "Encouragement for New Members' Wives in NAA," March 1952. "Anne S.," in Appendix A, appeared in the *AA Grapevine* in July 1949. All are copyright © The AA Grapevine, Inc. Reprinted with permission. Permission to reprint The AA Grapevine, Inc., copyrighted material in this publication does not in any way imply affiliation with or endorsement by either Alcoholics Anonymous or The AA Grapevine, Inc.

About the Author

MICHAEL FITZPATRICK is coauthor with William G. Borchert of *1000 Years of Sobriety* and is one of the leading historians and speakers in the field of alcoholism, specializing in the development of the Twelve Step movement. He owns what is possibly the largest audio archive related to the Twelve Step movement ever assembled, containing more than three thousand original reel-to-reel recordings of the voices of the men and women who pioneered the Twelve Step movement. Mike is in the process of digitizing these recordings, which are now being made available online at recoveryspeakers.org. Many of the transcripts in this book and recordings included in the accompanying CD and e-book are from this archive.

Mike lives in Chandler, Arizona, with his wife, Joy, and their three children. He and Joy work together to operate his business as a book broker and marketing consultant. Over the years Mike has written sales promotional pieces and training manuals for several major corporations. He has traveled extensively throughout the United States and Canada as a guest speaker and sales leader, motivating and inspiring his audiences with both his humor and his inspirational message of hope. His message to sales organizations is "attitude is everything!"

Hazelden, a national nonprofit organization founded in 1949, helps people reclaim their lives from the disease of addiction. Built on decades of knowledge and experience, Hazelden offers a comprehensive approach to addiction that addresses the full range of patient, family, and professional needs, including treatment and continuing care for youth and adults, research, higher learning, public education and advocacy, and publishing.

A life of recovery is lived "one day at a time." Hazelden publications, both educational and inspirational, support and strengthen lifelong recovery. In 1954, Hazelden published *Twenty-Four Hours a Day*, the first daily meditation book for recovering alcoholics, and Hazelden continues to publish works to inspire and guide individuals in treatment and recovery, and their loved ones. Professionals who work to prevent and treat addiction also turn to Hazelden for evidence-based curricula, informational materials, and videos for use in schools, treatment programs, and correctional programs.

Through published works, Hazelden extends the reach of hope, encouragement, help, and support to individuals, families, and communities affected by addiction and related issues.

For questions about Hazelden publications,
please call **800-328-9000**
or visit us online at **hazelden.org/bookstore.**